*Twayne's English Authors Series*

EDITOR OF THIS VOLUME

Kinley E. Roby

*Northeastern University*

*Sir Winston Churchill*

**TEAS 264**

Winston Churchill

# SIR WINSTON CHURCHILL

## By MANFRED WEIDHORN

*Yeshiva University*

**TWAYNE PUBLISHERS**
A Division of G. K. Hall & Co.
Boston, Massachusetts, U. S. A.

Copyright © 1979 by G. K. Hall & Co.

Published in 1979 by Twayne Publishers,
A Division of G. K. Hall & Co.
All Rights Reserved

Printed on permanent/durable acid-free paper and bound
in the United States of America

*First Printing*

For my sons, Aron and Eric.

**Library of Congress Cataloging in Publication Data**

Weidhorn, Manfred, 1931-
Sir Winston Churchill.

(Twayne's English authors series: TEAS 264)
Bibliography: p. 170–72
Includes index.
1.   Churchill, Winston Leonard Spencer, Sir, 1874-1965.   2.   Prime
ministers – Great Britain – Biography.
I.   Title.
DA566.9C5W367      941.082′092′4   [B]      79-580
ISBN 0-8057-6760-6

"Excluded from the Chamber, his voice could no longer be heard. Never mind! He had another weapon. He had a pen. He wrote for bread and life; for life and honor! And far and wide what he wrote was read. Thus he survived. He survived not to recover only, but to assault; not to assault, but to conquer. . . . The giant enemy towered up, brazen, and so far as we could see, invulnerable. It was at this moment . . . that the fierce old man was summoned to what was in fact the Dictatorship. He returned to power as Marius had returned to Rome; doubted by many, dreaded by all, but doom-sent, inevitable. . . . Happy the nation which when its fate quivers in the balance can find such a tyrant and such a champion."

— CHURCHILL (on Clemenceau)

"Their antique freedom has been asserted by the sword, and may be justified by the pen."

— GIBBON

"One thing is certain. You will be read, and annotated, and examined and compared."

— STANLEY BALDWIN to CHURCHILL

# Contents

# About the Author

Manfred Weidhorn was born in Vienna, Austria, and raised in Brooklyn, N.Y. After attending Columbia College and serving in the U.S. Army, he received the M.A. degree from the University of Wisconsin and the Ph.D. degree from Columbia University. He has taught at the University of Alabama and at Brooklyn College. Since 1963, he has been on the faculty of Yeshiva University, where he is now Professor of English. He has published some two dozen articles (mainly on Shakespeare, Milton, and Churchill) in such scholarly journals as Shakespeare Quarterly, Harvard Theological Review, Studies in Philology, Studies in English Literature, Centennial Review, Milton Quarterly, Quarterly Journal of Speech, and The Columbia Forum. He is also the author of four books: *Dreams In Seventeenth-Century English Literature* (1970); *Richard Lovelace* (TEAS #96; 1970); *Sword And Pen: A Survey Of The Writings Of Sir Winston Churchill* (1974); and (with Stanley Nass) *Turn Your Life Around* (1978).

# *Preface*

I undertake in this work a synoptic study. My subject is not the state of Churchill's mind in each of six phases but a setting forth of his basic ideas. My subsidiary subject is a consideration of the literary techniques that made him, irrespective of the content of his books, not just a politician tending to explain himself often but a writer meriting inclusion in the Twayne English Authors Series, even, perhaps, an artist. Instead of concentrating on his five major works, I scrutinize the whole corpus of books, speeches, and articles; instead of establishing how each of his major works differs from the other four, I isolate those ideas and literary devices which they share; instead of chronological order, I utilize topical order. Given the volume of Churchill's output and the space limitations in this series, I can present only small samples of Churchill's writing, and I can but indicate points of departure for future scholars working in depth in each of the areas touched on here. To do justice to the material, nearly every chapter would have to be expanded into a separate book—and someday no doubt will be.

I begin with a sketch of Churchill's life and writings and follow with a listing of his recurring themes and ideas on political power, diplomacy, indomitability, change, progress. A chapter is then devoted to one of his central concerns: the art of war and the example of Napoleon. Chapter 4 ascertains the extent to which Churchill's philosophy, despite an overlay of conventional moralizing, is suffused with Machiavellianism—the original, noble rather than the vulgar, misunderstood version. Another chapter sketches his outlook on the continents and races, the major world powers, the British character and mission. I survey next his handling of the *historian's* technical problems, matters like hindsight, foreshadowing, historical analogies, hypothetical conjecture, the portrayal of self as well as of leading personages, and the depiction of dramatic scenes. Chapter 7 deals with his handling of the *writer's* technical problems—such aspects of style as imagery, wit, diction, sentence structure. Stylistic lapses as well as triumphs are examined. The study is rounded off with a look at his place among British historians, his reputation, and his contribution to history and to literature.

The material in parentheses at the end of each quotation identifies the work, volume, and page number. The key to the abbreviations used for the titles will be found at the end of each entry in the bibliography of primary sources.

MANFRED WEIDHORN

*Yeshiva University*

# Chronology

1945    Victorious in war, defeated in general election.
1941-   Seven volumes of wartime speeches.
1946
1945-   Leader of the Opposition.
1951
1946    Important speeches at Fulton, Missouri, and Zurich.
1948-   *The Second World War*.
1953
1949-   Five volumes of postwar speeches.
1961
1951-   Conservative prime minister.
1955
1953    Knighted; Nobel Prize for literature.
1956-   *A History of the English-Speaking Peoples*.
1958
1965    Dies on January 25 at ninety.

## CHAPTER 1

# "An Endless Moving Picture": Life and Works

S IR Winston Leonard Spencer Churchill was born on November 30, 1874, in Blenheim Palace, Woodstock, Oxfordshire, to the younger son of the seventh duke of Marlborough. The blood of the Villiers, Sidneys, Spencers, and Churchills flowed in his veins, and the renowned warrior-diplomat of the early eighteenth century, John Churchill, first duke of Marlborough, was his ancestor. His maternal grandfather was an American millionaire, Leonard Jerome. He could hardly have had more impressive forebears.

His gregarious parents, Randolph and Jennie, moved in the highest social circles, and the child was left in the care of a nanny. Growing up as something of a rowdy, Winston was able to enjoy in school only history, geography, and English. Because of his blatant ignorance, the boy was spared the blessings of Greek and Latin studies and placed instead in a class devoted to the study of English composition. If he learned anything in school, it was how to write an English sentence, an invaluable and uncommon gift.

That history, geography, and English were to be his métier was not yet evident. His father, in fact, feared that the lad would become a "social wastrel," and his mother complained of his slangy English and his tendency to issue ultimata. Winston's erratic youth was due to a less than satisfactory home life. The brilliant if mercurial father, distracted, first, by his own quick rise in politics—he was for a short while a young leader of the House of Commons and concurrently chancellor of the exchequer—then, by his equally fast political demise, and, finally, by degenerative illness, never was close to the boy. Inferring, from Winston's preference for playing with toy soldiers rather than for studying, that the boy was not good for much, Randolph dispatched him into a military career. Thus a checkered scholastic record that included attendance at the elite school of Harrow and failure in various examinations was capped with entry into Sandhurst, the Royal Military Academy. At last Winston came upon a course of study and a life-style that he could enjoy—soldiering, strategy, and quasi-military comradeship.

In 1895, Churchill's twenty-first year, many important things happened to him. Both his awe-inspiring father and his beloved nanny died; he was graduated from Sandhurst; he had his first taste of warfare; and he began to write professionally. For, upon finishing his military training, he sought post-graduate and extramural education at the site of the Cuban-Spanish War and concurrently put his writing gift to use by obtaining an assignment from a London newspaper. The resulting series of dispatches was well received.

The newly commissioned cavalry officer next set off for his first tour of duty abroad, in India. He found the routine there congenial. At the same time, however, becoming aware that his lack of cultivation would handicap him if he was to make his way in the world, he undertook a program of reading—in history, religion, philosophy, and politics—and gave himself exercises in intellectual analysis. So responsive was his mind, so powerful already his need to express himself, that soon thereafter his reading stimulated a desire to give out as well as take in: without having digested too many literary classics, he began, abruptly, audaciously, to write a novel.

At this time, in 1897, Churchill aspired to enter his father's field of politics, and he privately expressed political sentiments in accord with his father's "Tory Democracy," that is, the Disraelian policy of welfare measures under Conservative auspices. But how would he reach such a career from his present inauspicious position as an impecunious subaltern? Even if he made a name for himself by achieving military glory, he faced the hurdle of lack of money. Now the writing, which had hitherto been a hobby or a pleasure, came to appear as the means of salvation. For one who as yet knew only military matters well, the writing would have to be intimately associated with real warmaking. When he heard, therefore, of an expedition being mounted in 1897 against troublesome border tribes in Northwest India, Churchill set aside the novel, volunteered for front-line service, and obtained another commission from a newspaper.

In Cuba he had merely been a foreign observer; here he was a combatant. A series of actions provided him with enough adventures, visits to exotic locales, and close brushes with death to furnish memories for a lifetime. The dispatches were again liked, but the absence of a by-line prevented him from reaping the expected renown. So, upon returning to his permanent station, he once again set aside the novel, this time for a work in a genre of writing that would become peculiarly his own—the war chronicle-memoir. Feverishly turning his dispatches into a book, he produced within five weeks the *Malakand Field Force*, which brought him a modicum of literary fame and the attention of the ruling elite of Britain. He had begun to make his mark.

He had also developed a modus operandi. In the following year, he obtained, after considerable wire-pulling, a similar assignment. Again as officer and correspondent, he joined Kitchener's expeditionary force. It descended into the Sudan to put out the last embers of a revolt which, nearly a generation earlier, had consumed the life of General Gordon. The result was, once more, participation in a series of adventures amid awesome natural scenery—and a book, *The River War*. A big book this time, for Churchill not only reworked his dispatches but also did considerable historical research in order to write the definitive version of the war.

History continued to provide the wars, and Churchill continued to obtain the writing commissions. In the following year came the Boer War, and, while the two volumes of only slightly revised dispatches did not make as much of an impact as his two previous books, his personal experiences finally brought him just the fame he had dreamed of. When an armored train on which he had embarked ran into an ambush, he took charge of the defense and managed to extricate a good part of the train. He himself was captured as a prisoner of war; but, after a short incarceration, he escaped from the prison barracks. The armored train incident, the prison break and disappearance, and, above all, his eventual reappearance, safe and sound, made him an international hero and a household name. Having garnered what he had joined the army for—adventure, fame, money—and something he had perhaps not planned

on—a vocation as a non-fiction author[1]—he could now leave
the military life for politics.

In 1899 he had made an abortive race for Parliament, but
when he repeated the attempt a year later as a young war hero,
the results were different. Before taking his seat in Commons,
he undertook a lecture tour in the British Isles and North
America in order to exploit his new-found fame and to develop
another new vocation, public speaking. Not so incidentally,
the tour brought in a large sum of money, which secured his
entry into politics. At the age of twenty-six, then, he passed the
first watershed of his fabulous career. In a series of calculated
steps and through massive willpower, audacity, and luck, he
had used his talents to bridge the gap, as few men do, between
his predicament and the goal of his aspirations. After detours
in military service, in remote lands, and in journalism and
book writing, he arrived at the place where his father had
gained his greatest triumphs and defeats—Westminster.

His luck and his resourcefulness continued. When he took
his seat in the Parliament of 1901, Churchill knew little besides military matters about the questions of the day. By
chance, military affairs were precisely at issue, and so the Parliamentary neophyte who was coincidentally the veteran of
the first phase of the Boer War could pronounce with authority. He proceeded to take a series of positions—lenity to the
Boers, opposition to increases in military expenditures, support of traditional British free trade policies—which im-
plemented his father's Tory democracy and his own vaguely
liberal sentiments. By 1904 he found himself isolated in the
Conservative party. What could he do now?

Soon after his entry into Parliament he had been given, on
the strength of his previous books and of his new interest in
politics, the task of writing a biography of his father. In this
massive work, which certified his reputation as a professional
author, he traced Randolph's growing radicalization. The
father had, for various reasons, stopped short of changing parties; the author-son, finding himself at a similar juncture, took
the leap. The result was hardly painful. The Liberals received
him with open arms and assigned him his first administrative
post, under-secretary for the colonies. During the next three
years, he played a modest role in the South African settlement

and busied himself with problems, large and small, of the African colonies.

If on the one hand, he was a proponent of the white man's burden and the British imperial mission, on the other hand, he opined that Britain should gather no more new territories and that the African natives were being ill treated by the British civil servants. Such liberal views were yoked with similar ones in the domestic sphere. He came to see that the problems caused by industrialization could not be solved merely by maintenance of free trade, as the older liberalism taught, but were so deeprooted as to require a reorientation of governance itself. The state, following the example of Bismarck's Germany, had to intervene in dozens of issues hitherto left to adjustment between employer and employee or between local government and the indigent. In 1908, as the new president of the Board of Trade, he began work on several specific welfare measures. He became associated with the outstanding "radical" in the party, David Lloyd George, as friend, colleague on the speaker's circuit, and abrasive defender of the socially innovative "People's Budget" of 1909. He published four volumes of brilliant speeches, frequently advised Prime Minister Asquith, and talked blithely of abolishing the reactionary House of Lords. Then he moved over to the Home Office, where, while still believing in–and exercising–capital punishment, he brought his reformist zeal to the prison system. Those were heady days of social ferment, and no doubt, in the words of the poet, "Bliss was it in that dawn to be alive."

For Churchill, however, the bloodless revolution came to a sudden halt when he was asked in 1911 to revitalize the admiralty. As first lord–the civilian, parliamentary head–of the admiralty, he immersed himself in matters like defense strategy, building the newest battleships, establishment of a naval air force, conversion from coal to oil, comparative fleet strengths, and, of course, the ominous, nascent problem of Germany. He who had long fought against increases in military budgets now threatened to resign if he did not obtain such increases. He pleaded for peace, called for international moratoria on warship construction, but prepared for the worst. When the worst did come, it found him ready. He wisely sent the fleet to its battle station during the height of the crisis that initiated World War I. The necessary measures having been taken in the preceding three years, Britain retained her venerable naval supremacy. After several mishaps, she won a victory in the South Atlantic that ended Germany's short-lived role as an active sea power.

The Allies, as he wrote, could lose the war on the seas but win it only on the ground, and, as 1914 ended, Churchill became preoccupied with the problem of the western front. Like Lloyd George, he saw that a stalemate had been achieved along the trenches and that, because of modern firepower, the offensive needed a superiority of manpower that neither side could approximate. If the Allies resorted instead to an attack on the Dardanelles, they could, he reasoned, utilize their vast sea power and reap numerous military and political advantages. But the expedition that was finally mounted in 1915 turned out to be a debacle. Although Churchill insisted then and ever after that it had not been carried out in the form in which he had envisioned it, someone had to be the scapegoat, and what better candidate than he, who had been its vocal champion and who had, in any case, managed since his entry into politics to irritate even more people than had Lloyd George?

After a short stint in a sinecure position, Churchill returned to the army, eventually serving for a few months as a battalion commander on the front in France. Though glad to be free of political intrigue, he kept an ear cocked on developments in Westminster. When Lloyd George finally displaced Asquith as prime minister, Churchill was, after a decent interval, appointed minister of munitions. At war's end, he moved to the War Office and, two years later, to the Colonial Office. In these three posts, he accomplished many good things, like providing a munitions surplus, rationalizing the demobilization process, and making political settlements (of sorts) in Ireland and in the Middle East, but the great opportunity of which he had long dreamed—of leading a victorious military force or even of becoming wartime prime minister—had apparently drowned in the rough waters off Gallipoli. Postwar actions, like coordinating the fruitless Allied intervention in Bolshevik Russia or sending ultimata to Turkey, might well have seemed to observers a comic replay of his tragic wartime failure, desperate last attempts to be a modern Napoleon.

When in 1922 the Lloyd George government fell, partly as a

result of (as it then seemed) Churchill's bellicosity, the political picture struck the erstwhile "radical" as chaotic. Abroad, Bolshevism, having survived its baptism of fire in Russia, appeared ready to cross national boundaries into lands severely distressed by the Great War. At home, unemployment, labor militancy, and the rising socialist movement were certain to be easy prey for alien dogmas and conspirators. The Liberal party, which Churchill had celebrated in his reformist days as the bulwark against revolutionary solutions, was riven into the Lloyd George and Asquith wings, and Churchill, while advocating a few liberal measures, found himself close to neither wing but moving to the right. Worst of all, for the first and only time in his career, he experienced a series of consecutive election defeats at the hands of differing constituencies and under different, and unconventional, party labels. If in 1915-1916, he had been out of the government, in 1922-1924, he was out of Parliament itself and outside the traditional party system as well. He busied himself with work on *The World Crisis,* his large, by turns eloquent, moving, long-winded, always idiosyncratic and self-justifying version of the war.

But Churchill was still a political factor to be reckoned with. His political exile and drift ended with a return to Parliament, to the Conservative party, and, concurrently, to government office. Prime Minister Baldwin in 1924, in one of the many surprises in Churchill's roller-coaster career, made Churchill chancellor of the exchequer. History has not adjudged his five years at this post to be memorable. By bringing Britain back to the gold standard and following, according to the economic wisdom of the day, a deflationary policy, he generated a confrontation with the coal miners which led to the general strike of 1926.

He behaved now like a reactionary not only on domestic matters. When, in 1929, the first Labor government in British history proposed to grant India a measure of autonomy, Churchill arose to fight a bitter rearguard action. In this antiquated posture, he battled not only Laborites and Liberals but even most fellow Conservatives, who could see the handwriting on the wall, and in 1931, he resigned his place in the Conservative shadow cabinet. Now he entered upon his longest period of exile, in many ways an embittered, querulous, anachronistic old politician whom history had bypassed. The splendor of the dawn, of adventure, reform, daring, was but a lost dream. Dur-

ing the following decade, Churchill, in the "political wilderness" over the question of India, then rearmament, then the
abdication, and lastly appeasement, had much leisure. While
Roosevelt and Hitler approached the seats of power and their
rendezvous with destiny, Churchill spent his time painting,
bricklaying, writing a charming brief autobiography, sketches
of contemporary prominent personages, or the large, definitive biography of his ancestor, Marlborough—and making an
occasional irritating speech on Germany.

Belles-lettres might well have displaced politics for good,
were it not for the sound of decidedly different drummers in
Germany. The ascendancy of the Nazis and the consequent
accelerated rearming of the Germans caused Churchill to
warn of growing dangers. He was at first almost alone. His
pugnacity on various foreign policy issues throughout his
career, his frequent changes of party and position, his militancy against the trade unions, his bullheadedness on India,
his apparently heartless fiscal policy during the Depression,
his moral blinkers on the Ethiopian, Manchurian, and Spanish
questions, his sentimental and archaic position on the abdication crisis—all had stamped him as a reactionary, a warmonger,
an irresponsible, ambitious, or irrational rogue. Undaunted,
Churchill went his way, continuing, in Parliament, to issue
warnings and, at home, to study the remote past. Upon finishing *Marlborough*, he began work on *A History of the English-Speaking Peoples*. If his career had missed its expected
climax and if the modern century was, as he came increasingly
to feel, a dispiriting age in permanent crisis, he at least had
found in these delvings into the past his intellectual air-raid
shelter.

As the menace of Hitler became evident to everyone, however, Churchill's status changed from that of pariah to prophet.
If war was indeed coming, he had foreseen the danger and
suggested preventive measures; the "old warhorse" (Stalin's
term) would in any case be needed. First Labor moved closer
to him, and then, with even Chamberlain sensing the need—or
at least the political pulse—the commencement of hostilities
returned Churchill to his old job at the Admiralty.

His accomplishments in his brief second turn at the Admiralty were, to say the least, not prodigious, but his predisposi-
tion for making war and his record of relative accuracy through

the previous years on the question of Hitler had built up a momentum which catapulted him into the prime ministership during the very hours in which the German blitzkrieg turned from the Scandinavian to the Low Countries and France. He seemed to many the only man for the job at that terrible juncture. At last the long postponed climax of his life manifested itself, after he had perhaps given up on it. There followed a year, 1940, which he could barely have dreamed of, which he would treasure in the remaining quarter century of life left him as his greatest, and which is truly his best claim to immortality. Britain was in a parlous state: alone and insufficiently armed, she faced a juggernaut. But she was led by someone who would not—unlike Lloyd George and others—parley or capitulate, who long had celebrated fighting for lost causes, who could express his determination with unequaled fervor, and who inspired his people with his eminent indomitability.[2]

The quest for survival was soon replaced by the quest for victory, a task made much easier by Hitler's commencing hostilities with Russia in June and America in December of 1941. These fateful decisions brought cobelligerents into the field, and Churchill, like his ancestor, proceeded to weave together a grand alliance. Still, heroic leadership in adversity and successful grand diplomacy were unfortunately not enough. After nearly three years of unrelieved defeats and evacuations, of blitzkrieg from the air and sinkings from undersea, the British people, if not their rejuvenated leader, had grown weary of the firing line. Churchill faced offensives on the home front. Having turned back the Luftwaffe and U-boats, he now had to fend off two votes of censure in 1942 and to make minimal gestures toward postwar reform. Only just in time to save his political life came the Allied landings in North Africa, the British victory at El Alamein, and the inception of a period of three years filled with the long deferred and almost unrelieved joys of invasions and victories.

If matters in the military and domestic spheres now improved greatly, in the diplomatic sphere, paradoxically, they did not. Allies had to be deferred to—as Marlborough, and through him Churchill, well knew—the more so as their frontline commitments grew. At first, after many debates with the Russians and Americans, both of whom were eager for a

prompt second front, Churchill had had his way; in lieu of operations in the West, two years were spent in the Mediterranean theater. He not only delayed the second front, he also
helped ensure its success. Just as in World War I he played a
major role in the development of the tank and the warplane, so
now were the Normandy landings eased in part by virtue of
his midwifery of the Mulberry artificial harbor and the tank
landing craft.

But Churchill could not match his achievements in war
technology with achievements in war diplomacy. When the
second front did come in 1944, the Russians, having done a
thorough job of bleeding the Germans white, and the Americans, having built up a large preponderance in military might,
now had the moral and political authority that comes with
power. Britain was a helpful albeit no longer unexpendable
ally. Churchill found himself at conferences abroad left out of
an occasional summit meeting between the president and Stalin or being forced to share the spotlight with such men
as—the more galling as he never could be persuaded to regard
Asians as the peers of Europeans or China as a major power—Chiang Kaishek. His innovations in military strategy and
in foreign policy now consisted of his urging, in vain, the cap-
ture of Vienna and Berlin by Anglo-American rather than Russian forces and of his sending British troops to Greece against
local Communists—ideas and actions which alienated him
from the Americans and endeared him even less to the Russians. The Cold War had begun, and, more painful, the all too
short and mainly illusory Anglo-American special relationship
had ended. Worst of all, at this critical moment of the rending
of the wartime alliances, victory in Europe was twinned with a
smashing defeat at the voting booth. Here was another surprising turnabout in, and one of the greatest setbacks of, Churchill's long career. The British people expected their wartime
sacrifices to be followed by social reconstruction, and Churchill simply was not—had not been for thirty five years—the
man for such a task.

Now came a long sunset, with clouds. Churchill spent the
first postwar years writing the by then obligatory war
memoirs, acting as mediocre leader of the Opposition, and
making important speeches as Europe's first citizen. He
warned men about the designs of his erstwhile ally, Stalin,

even as he had warned them about Hitler. At the same time, he believed that war would be avoided through alliances and rearming, both of which soon materialized. He also strongly urged a United Europe movement. On domestic matters, his carping at the Attlee administration's monumental inauguration of the welfare state was not on the level of his pronouncements on international affairs.

When his party returned to power in 1951, he had suffered several strokes which impaired his powers of speech and his mental agility. His record as peacetime prime minister was neither disastrous nor impressive. He ceased to talk of the United Europe movement because it was unpopular at home. He moderated his attitudes toward the trade unions and the Russians; in the last two years of his ministry, in fact, he called for summit meetings with the post-Stalinist Russian leaders and spoke optimistically of détente. His eightieth birthday in 1954 was an unprecedented national celebration. The Conservatives, however, grew restive under his lethargic leadership, and he was finally prevailed upon to step down in April, 1955.

Though retaining his seat in the House, he at first spent much of his time putting his literary house in order: revising and publishing the *History*, writing an epilogue to the *Second World War*, reissuing earlier works with new prefaces. His literary labors appear to have ceased altogether in 1957. In the last eight years of his life, a pall of melancholy, irritability, and senility descended upon him—a condition poignant when one considers that he led one of the most active and exciting of lives. In 1964, he relinquished his seat in the House, and, soon after passing his ninetieth birthday, he died, in January, 1965. He was given a state funeral probably unequaled since the one for the duke of Wellington, conqueror of Napoleon, a century earlier. He was buried alongside his parents and relatives in the humble village church of Bladon, a couple of miles from his birthplace in Blenheim Palace. But on the pavement near the entrance of Westminster Abbey was later placed a stone which simply said, "REMEMBER WINSTON CHURCHILL."

## CHAPTER 2

# "A Curious Education": The SemiIntellectual

## I  The Reader

WHEN his first book, the nonfictional *Malakand Field Force,* was concluded, Churchill was torn between the desire to resume work on his novel, *Savrola*, and the compulsion to read. As he put it picturesquely, in the language of a nascent politician, "the balance between Imports and Exports must be maintained." Working on the *Randolph Churchill* a few years later, he again faced the paradox that his mind was empty, for he was so busy writing that he had no time to read. All writers understand his plight; no one can be a writer for long who does not read, yet reading consumes much precious time. Still, notwithstanding his busy life in journalism and politics (and sometimes in military affairs), Churchill managed to do quite a bit of reading. Much of it was, to be sure, on history and politics, but not all of it.

Churchill's interest in books in general and literature in particular is a curious subject. Unlike most prominent British politicians, he was, despite being the grandson of a duke, not entirely a part of the old-boy network: he had not attended Oxbridge or indeed any university. His education was patchy. After delighted exposure to English literature (mainly Shakespeare, Milton, Macaulay) in his early school years came a period of intellectual torpor from which he at last tried to awaken himself during his army days in India. He imposed on himself a regimen of study centered on works of politics and history (Macaulay and Gibbon, Plato and Aristotle, Adam Smith and Darwin). His readings in imaginative literature were less methodical. While composing *Savrola* he tried to learn his craft by reading a lot of Kipling, some Hardy, Stevenson, Meredith, Crane, Mrs. Ward—that is, the prominent novelists of the day. A special perennial taste was Mark Twain. He reveled in his writings by the age of twelve. Tom Sawyer and Huck Finn symbolized America. His first hobby, long kept up, was collecting various editions of the American master.[1]

Young Churchill became, according to his friend the old poet W. S. Blunt, a rapid and voracious reader of books, but with limited range, and, despite his autodidacticism, he remained a clever and brilliant rather than intellectual and erudite man. Churchill himself thought, in old age, that reading had prepared him for his career as author and politician but that that double career, ironically, had limited the time for, and scope of, his reading; though he had written much, his life had been too full of activities to enable him to read much. In that same old age, however, with his writing and political careers nearly over and with difficulty in concentrating on official duties as P.M., he read many Victorian novels for the first time and enjoyed them, especially Trollope's political novels. Though he thought it droll that his education in the Victorian novel began at eighty, one can readily see nostalgia and regression on the part of the old man looking back to his beginnings in that era, to a vanished world.[2]

It is curious that his tendencies to mythicize and romanticize, to seek the heroic and the ideal, should not have impelled Churchill more deeply into reading fiction throughout his life. Both in youth and in old age, he had the understanding which distinguishes the intellectual from the casual reader—that one should not ignore the importance of the "claims of literature and language," of reading books, and of a knowledge of the past; that it is better "to understand one book than to have read a hundred"; that the classics should not be read "hurriedly or at an immature period of development" or as a result of school assignments for vacation periods; that the more one reads, the more one grows uncomfortably aware of all that one has not, and never will, read; that, while he would apply with "moderation" the principle of reading an old book whenever a new one appears, "it is a great mistake to live entirely in the present"; and that it is unfortunate that men no longer read the classics (*SoP*, 109, 124). Like any compulsive reader, he had a horror of wasting a day and believed that even to read a fine book not read before was something productive.[3]

He even boasted once that the one thing he really knew was

literature and what constituted a good book. At various times in his career he confidently singled out for praise Disraeli's *Sybil*, Upton Sinclair's *The Jungle*, Shaw's *Major Barbara*, and T. E. Lawrence's *Seven Pillars of Wisdom* (which he ranked with what he considered the greatest English books, *Pilgrim's Progress, Robinson Crusoe,* and *Gulliver's Travels*).

He wrote one passage on books which could only have come from a confirmed believer in the delights of reading. While it owes a lot to Bacon, it has a lovely lilt of its own:

"What shall I do with all my books?" was the question; and the answer, "Read them," sobered the questioner. But if you cannot read them, at any rate handle them and, as it were, fondle them. Peer into them. Let them fall open where they will. Read on from the first sentence that arrests the eye. Then turn to another. Make a voyage of discovery, taking soundings of uncharted seas. Set them back on their shelves with your own hands. Arrange them on your own plan, so that if you do not know what is in them, you at least know where they are. If they cannot be your friends, let them at any rate be your acquaintances. If they cannot enter the circle of your life, do not deny them at least a nod of recognition. . . . It is a great pity to read a book too soon in life. The first impression is the one that counts. . . . Young people should be careful in their reading, as old people in eating their food. They should not eat too much. They should chew it well (*ATS*, 300).[4]

Yet Churchill had a heavy touch with literature. When Asquith, he once said—not without scorn and pity—turned from politics to reading and other interests, he closed the door and would have no shop talk. Not so Churchill. He needed to politicize everything. Consequently he sought in literary works their relevance to social issues. His patriotism mingled with his response to literature as to everything else. Congratulating his brother on being accepted to Oxford, he remarked on the opportunity to study there "the glorious classics of our own language." His political orientation also prompted him to remark that to love the English language is not only to preserve "our literature" but also to make us members of that great English-speaking world with whom man's future "will largely rest." Significant therefore is his description of a work he often referred to, *Sybil*: it was one of Disraeli's most remarkable novels, "a work of fiction that was not only a literary but also a political event."[5]

Other novels to which he responded—or about which he at

least wrote – likewise had ramifications in the world of affairs. He rarely comments on anything having to do with the inner life. When a young man fighting at Lloyd George's side on behalf of the welfare measures proposed by the New Liberals, Churchill wrote (in 1906) a book review of Upton Sinclair's muckraking novel, *The Jungle*. He saw it as part of the reformers' attempt to turn the American Democratic party into a Socialist one. He thought that the book, even if, unlike the laborious contemporary nonfictional muckraking volumes, it was only one-tenth true, did great service in exposing corruption, especially in American politics, and in depicting a human tragedy. He also wondered, characteristically, whether such extreme corruption could be modified by state action at all.

Years later, worried about Hitler, he cited Sinclair Lewis's *It Can't Happen Here* (about the coming of Fascism to America) for offering, as he thought, a necessary warning. His mind was also diverted at the juncture of literature with military matters. Reading Steinbeck's *The Moon Is Down* (a novel about the very war in which Churchill himself was a leader), he borrowed from it an idea for underground dynamite work. He not only sought out political novels but applied political standards universally. When, during a wartime siege of pneumonia, *Pride and Prejudice* was read to him, no doubt as a distraction from the cares of office, it elicited a comment only too heavily shaped by his current interests: "What calm lives they had, those people! No worries about the French Revolution, or the crashing struggle of the Napoleonic Wars" (*SWW*, V, 425) – an adverse judgment apparently both on the characters and on their author. The ideological blinders of his antipacifism, like his obliviousness to a wider vision of life, to anything transcending politics and patriotism, caused him sometimes to operate unwittingly according to the canons of socialist realism and resulted in, for instance, his dismissal (in old age) of an elegiac wartime poem as defeatist stuff.[6]

In early 1933, a time of economic and political dislocations, of the fateful entry into leadership positions of Roosevelt and Hitler, Churchill, in the political wilderness but introduced by the editor as the holder of more cabinet posts than anyone else living and as a colorful, brilliant man, undertook (in conjunction with a ghost writer) a series in the newspaper the *News of the World*, "The World's Great Stories Retold by Winston

Churchill." The title is misleading, albeit in a predictable manner, for Churchill, with his uneven acquaintance with literature, fervid patriotism, and numerous archaic traits, understood by the "world's great stories" mainly nineteenth century British novels. These pieces contain little literary analysis, consisting rather of straightforward, unimaginative synopses of plot, with only a rare reflection or introductory comment, bearing, of course, in some way on politics—the entrenched system of slavery (*Uncle Tom's Cabin*), sidelights on early Victorian justice (*The Moonstone*), the contrast between the British evolutionary tradition and French political rigidity and the fact that the French Revolution did clear the way for the onward march of man (*A Tale of Two Cities*).

Even a paraphrase of the story of Moses shows his need to politicize everything; the scriptural story is made comprehensible to a student of modern politics and applicable to current economic problems. Thus the slaughter of the first born was a combination of anti-Semitism (like the modern kind) and the practice of birth control to meet the problem of unemployment. Moses's slaying of an Egyptian struck "Egyptian public opinion"—"there is always public opinion where there is the slightest pretence of civilization"—as a "final proof that the weakness of the government towards these overweening strangers and intruders had reached its limit. At any rate Pharaoh—which is as good a name as any other for the governing classes at any time under any system—acted." Both Pharaoh's decreeing death on the murderer and the fleeing of the murderer "conformed to modern procedure." Moses's exile was necessary for meditation in isolation (as it is for any prophet) on the "strong impressions of a complex society" which he had received. Later, flanked by Aaron, "a competent orator, some man used to putting cases and dealing in high affairs," Moses begins his siege of the Court. Pharaoh's reactions are "modern" (*ATS*, 286-88).

## II  *The Uses of Literature*

What, then, did Churchill read? He certainly knew his English Bible and Shakespeare, both of which, among the classics of the English language, he regarded as great sources of "imagination and strength." Shakespeare was clearly important to him, if we judge by the number of quotations and allusions in his writings. (A fourth or a third of his plays are drawn upon—*Hamlet* often, *Lear, Othello, Antony, Coriolanus*, and the sonnets never.) Churchill indeed differs from most other modern world leaders in having been, like earlier British statesmen, steeped in the Bible. It is amusing to see in the *Second World War* biblical quotations, citations, or rhythms crop up in the midst of workaday telegrams with generals and statesmen. In the wake of a Wavell victory, a curious exchange took place: *"Prime Minister to General Wavell.* St. Matthew, Chapter VII, verse 7. *General Wavell to Prime Minister.* St. James, Chapter I, verse 17" (*SWW*, II, 615). Not exactly your customary governmental missive! At various times he also referred Macmillan and Roosevelt to Matthew vii:16, xvii:4, and John xiv:1-4—in the latter case worrying over "unintended profanity."

Then came, more or less in order of decreasing frequency, Kipling, Pope (especially the *Essay on Man*), Macaulay, Burke, Tennyson, Milton, Bunyan, Byron (from whom he took the phrase "united nations"), Swift, Dryden, and Carlyle. Occasionally quoted or referred to are Bacon (mainly in the *Randolph Churchill*), Defoe, Dr. Johnson, Gibbon, Burns, Omar Khayyam, Dickens, Mill, Clough, Disraeli. Non-literary sources of quotations are Bismarck, Gladstone, Lecky, Bagehot, Clemenceau, Admiral Fisher, the American Constitution and Declaration of Independence, the Federalist Papers, some French and German proverbs, and, of course, Napoleon. Even less often referred to are Homer, Herodotus, Thucydides, Greek Tragedy (in general), Virgil, Caesar (as author), Plutarch, Dante, Donne, Marvell, Addison, Grey, Crabbe, Blake, Coleridge, Jane Austen, Ruskin, Lewis Carroll, A. C. Doyle, Stevenson, Wells, Shaw, Brooke, Sassoon, C. S. Forester.

What is interesting about this list is that: (a) It is mainly British; except for rare and not very learned references to Twain, Whitman (whose lines on fruition having to be followed by greater struggle he "always liked"), Longfellow (whom he often recited in old age), Emerson, H. B. Stowe, O. W. Holmes, Sinclair Lewis, Upton Sinclair; to Buffon, Hugo, Balzac, Verne; to Goethe, Schopenhauer, Nietzsche, and Schiller, Churchill was oblivious to the literatures of other peoples; (b) It excludes almost as many important British writers as it includes; there is, for example, no writer more "modern" and less political than Wells, Shaw, Kipling, that is, of the great generation of his coevals which flourished in the 1910s and 1920s. (A pair of vague references in the 1930s—"Freudian fantasies," "inferiority complexes"—bespeak no acquaintance with the Viennese master's writings.) (c) His quotations are fairly constant throughout his career; Shakespeare, Kipling, Burke are as often referred to in the first books as in the last. Nor are there any changes in emphases. Churchill seems either to have read nothing new or to have been possessed only by what he read as a young man.

Of interest also is the use of his reading in his own writing. Churchill's first published books contain numerous literary epigraphs, quotations (including some in Latin), and references, but the major influence appears to be only *Bartlett's Quotations*. Conventional references to Greek Tragedy throughout his life—whether he discusses the Dardanelles expedition, the story of C. S. Parnell, the British assault on the French fleet in 1940, or, inevitably, Greece's role in either World War—show little acquaintance with the original.[8] The *World Crisis*, on the other hand, exhibits evidence of a close reading of *Paradise Lost II* in his interesting if simplistic presentation of a Bolshevik conclave on the question of peace negotiations with Germany. Here is a "new debate in Pandemonium," with Trotsky cast as Moloch urging renewal of the war and swaying the assembled until "the calm sober voice of Lenin rallied them to their duty in a Belial discourse of 18 theses. 'I should be much for open war, O Peers, / As not behind in hate' " (*WC*, V, 75).[9] (Book I of Milton's epic had been exploited in the early pages of the *River War*.) Another heavy literary influence, at least in the pages on the Russian Revolution, was Edmund Burke (as Shaw even indicated to Stalin): Churchill standing vis-à-vis Russia in the years 1917-22 rather as did Burke vis-à-vis France in 1789-91, the mawkish lines on Czar Nicholas II clearly echo Burke's famous, or infamous, lines on Marie Antoinette.

In the *Marlborough*, there are few literary quotations and these mainly from the writers of the age under discussion—Dryden, Pope, Addison, Swift. Three of these masters of English literature appear in roles for which they are perhaps not suited—as political witnesses. Churchill is at pains to refute the attacks on his hero by contemporary Tories like Pope and Swift, attacks amplified by later Whigs like Thackeray and Macaulay. The latter historian, especially, though providing Churchill's favorite reading matter at an early age, is the *bête noir* of Volume I, and Churchill resorts to ad hominem arguments against him. Curiously enough, Churchill's next work (in order of composition, not of publication), the *History*, is most reminiscent of Macaulay's *History of England*, which he described as "great" though prejudiced, erratic, and naive about progress. In the *History*, the few literary contributions of England he deigns to notice are mainly those of the Augustan greats, an acquaintance no doubt established or renewed by his earlier delving into the Marlborough story. This work contains as well Churchill's only written observations on Shakespeare, whose "magic finger touches in succession most of the peaks of English history and lights them with the sunrise so that all can see them standing out above the mountainous disorder" (*HESP*, I, 192). He seems to, on the whole, accept Shakespeare's version of fifteenth-century English history.

At this time also, in the 1930s, the decade of his belles lettres, Churchill made a few ventures into literary criticism (besides the plot paraphrases), notably in his essay on Shaw. He saw Shaw as in every way—wit, dialogue, themes, construction, comprehension—a more satisfying Oscar Wilde. Shaw made two innovations: he turned his back on the "well-made play," and he made drama out of the interplay of argument and argument rather than of character and character or character and circumstance. "His ideas become personages, and fight among themselves, sometimes with intense dramatic effect. His human beings are there for what they are to say, not for what they are to be or do. Yet they live." Another technique involves a deliberate fickleness in treatment; various individuals or groups—the Salvation Army, the Irish, Joan of Arc—are portrayed at first sympathetically and then ridiculed, excoriated, dismissed. "The Shavian cow has no sooner yielded its record milking than it kicks the pail over the thirsty and admiring milker." Of individual plays, he praises *Major*

*Barbara* for remaining, after twenty years of unparalleled dislocations and social change, the "very acme of modernity"
(*GC*, 38, 40).

The exact nature of the influence of literature on Churchill's
writings is of interest mainly to literary scholars and Churchill
specialists; of more universal interest is the influence of literature on Churchill's imagination and thereby on his actions and
on the course of events. He early came to see some of his experiences through the spectacles of literature. The building of
the Desert Railway in the River War was a tale containing matter of romance for the "pen of Kipling" (*RW* I, 277). Life and
literature mingled curiously in the Boer War: He knew how far
he had come when, as an escaped prisoner of war in hiding, he
read Stevenson's *Kidnapped*, and its description of Balfour's
escape "awakened sensations with which I was only too familiar" (*MEL*, 290). And in World War I he used Burns's poetry to
soothe the Scotsmen in the battalion he commanded.

More momentous and public was the occasion when poetry,
with Churchill's help, entered on the stage of history and in-
fused events with a special meaning. In early 1941, Roosevelt,
in encouraging British endurance, sent Churchill the Longfellow lines, "Sail on, O ship of State! / . . . Humanity . . . / Is
hanging breathless on thy fate!" In doing so, he wrote, "This
verse applies to your people as it does to us." Churchill broad-
cast the lines, with their encouraging hint, to the world and
reapplied them to the donor nation. (Later he wrote in his
memoirs that "these splendid lines were an inspiration.") In a
speech of a few months later he harked back to the poem and
added: "I have some other lines which are less well known
but which seem apt and appropriate to our fortunes tonight,
and I believe they will be so judged wherever the English
language is spoken" (*SWW*, 26, 28, 237). He quoted two stan-
zas from a poem by Clough ending "But westward, look, the
land is bright."

There is not likely to have been another case in history of
two wartime leaders signaling to the world a message of
spiritual communion and potential alliance by means of an exchange of lines of poetry. That each patriotically quoted from
his own literature but both in the same language was made
possible by the existence of a common English literary tradition, of an "English-speaking" community. The exchange was

also made possible by the cultivation of the two leaders, particularly by Churchill's ability to find in a relatively obscure poem precisely the line that fitted the occasion and answered Roosevelt. Poetry not as counters in witty combat, as ornament for intellectual dinner conversation, as matter for leisure-time reading, or even as the means of self discovery but as an important kind of public statement, as the ultimate form of expression at a major juncture of history, and as a medium conveying nuances beyond the reach of discursive prose—poetry had then entered into the public communications of political leaders. More relevant than that, literature cannot become. Who is to say that the reading a man—even a politician—does at any period in his life may not come back years later to haunt, or inspire, him—and millions besides him?

# CHAPTER 3

# *"Always the Same Set of Songs"*: *Topoi*

IN one of his World War II speeches, Churchill said apropos
his readiness to go to any place to meet with Allied or neutral leaders, "I have not hesitated to travel from Court to Court
like a wandering minstrel, always with the same song to
sing—or the same set of songs" (*DoL,* 220). Whether or not this
elfish simile applies to his wartime diplomacy and strategy, it
clearly describes the continuity in his writings. Despite the
length of his authorial career and the vast growth in his experiences, themes in the early works are still vigorously forwarded in the last ones, often in unaltered form. Some of these
are trivial, like the tired proverb with which he coyly dismissed
amatory maters: love and marriage not being a subject of
interest to him as a writer, he tersely says of Savrola, of the
Sudanese soldiers and the women left behind by the routed
Dervishes, of himself, of Marlborough, of Martin Luther, that
they "married and lived happily ever afterwards." Because of
this indifference to the inner life, potentially interesting
themes remain undeveloped; of such a nature are the brief
remarks in several of his books, with reference to the Mahdi,
Marlborough, Randolph Churchill, and, implicitly, himself, on
a child's early independence in the absence of a forceful
father.

Some are turns of thought or part concept and part figure of
speech, like the recurring tableau of the civilized jolting the
primitive: in telling in the *River War* about a railway work-
shop sending black smoke into the "African sky," Churchill
wrote, "the malodorous incense of civilization was offered to
the startled gods of Egypt" (*RW,* I, 290). This sentence, clearly
modeled on Gibbon's remark that in Rome under Gratian "the
delicacy of the Christians was offended by the fumes of
idolatrous sacrifice," was found by some to be exaggerated or
ridiculous. But its metaphysical conceit treats the offensive

industrial smoke as though it were a religious offering, and modern civilization indeed rests on worship of the machine; the incongruity of machinery in backward Africa is nicely rendered by the adjective "startled."

A decade later, he described the jarring impact of modern civilization on primitive men, not on the gods they worship: the British Uganda railway is an "iron fact grinding along through the jungle and the plain, waking with its whistles the silences of the Nyanza, and startling the tribes out of their primordial nakedness" (*AJ*, 5). After three more decades, the eclipse of religion by technology is described less dramatically: "The factory whistle, with its summons to mass production, is replacing the call to prayer" in Moslem countries.[1] Yet two more decades later, the idea (in its Uganda version) is repeated, albeit subtly modified: the mingling in Australia of the most primitive and the most advanced can be an ominous reminder of the mixed blessings of progress: "The silence of the bush and the loneliness of the desert are only disturbed by the passing of some transcontinental express, the whirr of a boomerang, or the drone of a pilotless missile" (*HESP*, IV, 94). Through a span of exactly sixty years and through changes in style, Churchill's ideas abided, in their vividly sensuous and concrete form, and one may well ask Yeats's philosophical question, "Saw I an old man young / Or young man old?"

## I   *Politics*

Churchill's main themes are on the three topics which constituted virtually his only interests—politics, war, history. One refrain is, like the one on marriage, little more than a truism or cliché but reveals something of the function Churchill assigns to his writing: "Each man has his tale to tell." This is his reply to the reader's implicit question as to the provenance and the authoritativeness of the material in each book. Churchill presents most of his works as one man's contribution to, rather than a definitive version of, history. Historians will impose design and explain everything, but those who lived through events have their own impressions and know some of the horrors of experience. "Each man saw the world along his lance, under his guard, or through the back sight of his pistol" (*RW*, II, 137). Sometimes "every trench, every mound," or an army, a "nation or group of nations has its own tale to tell" (*HESP*, I,

xviii). In the Boer War "many men must tell their tale before
any general account" or even "the whole true account of a
single action" (L, 406; IH, 133) can be written. His function as
writer is to tell one of those tales; if he presumes to give the
definitive version of the River War as well as of the careers of
Randolph Churchill and Marlborough, he more commonly
presents one man's view of a war in the *Malakand*, the Boer
War books, the *World Crisis*, and the *Second World War*, and
one man's version of the tale of the English-speaking peoples.

Since each individual or group has his or its perspective, the
wise historian will be slow to jump to conclusions. Churchill
quotes some lines from Crabbe to the effect that, if we retrace
all of a man's deeds, nothing in his life will seem abrupt or
strange. In most of his writings, Churchill appeals for sympathetic identification and urges reader or political opposition
to "only utilize that valuable gift of putting themselves in imagination in the position of others" (*LSP*, 142). Hence, as a
young officer, he remarked that it is "easy to criticize with
complete knowledge, in safety, and at leisure the actions of
men done at hazard in a moment" (*RW*, II, 234); as a young patriot
felt not "unkindly" to a turncoat and time-server in the Boer
War, for a "weak man is a pitiful object in times of trouble,"
and Britons living in South Africa or even assisting the Boer
ambulances "had been placed in situations which do not come
to men in quiet times . . . and [been] torn by so many conflicting emotions that they must be judged very tolerantly" (*IH*,
230; *L*, 170-71); as a young radical drew a moving portrait of
the casual unskilled laborer holding miscellaneous insecure
jobs even in the best of times and being, with his family, the
victim of circumstances; and as an old man, while declaring
Munich a total defeat, made clear that "I have deeply understood from personal experiences of my own in a similar crisis
the stress and strain [Chamberlain] has had to bear" (*BST*, 55).
Not only did he "understand" the obsessive American feelings against Communist China—though not China's like feelings against the West!—but he took the larger leap into the
minds of the Russians to "see the problem as they see it" (*UA*,
114).

Aware of the vanity of power or the mockery of high command in modern war, Churchill sympathized even with those
on the enemy side and would make "every allowance" for
them; "it is easy for critics to recount lost opportunities" (*WC*,

VI, 376). He placed on the reader of the correspondence of the czar and the kaiser the burden of asking himself, before passing judgment, if he could have avoided the errors of the one and the crimes of the other, especially in such pampered situations. His early remark that only those who have undergone great battles can imagine what the Dervishes experienced turns into an injunction often iterated in the later war memoirs. In discussing, for instance, the failures of General Gamelin or Premier Laval, he said, "[Gamelin] was a patriotic, well meaning man and skilled in his profession, and no doubt he has his tale to tell. . . . One can certainly understand M. Laval's point of view at this time" (*SWW*, II, 49; *I*, 183). French fears of Germany would be clearer if Britons imagined themselves being invaded four times in a century, or Italian suspicions about British outrage over Ethiopia are explicable in terms of the relatively recent British acquisition of the Sudan and South Africa. Churchill suggested to the Germans that in warning Britain of approaching peril, he did only what Hitler "had [he] been in my position" (*SbS*, 142) would have done—Churchill having already remarked that, given Germany's predicament, Hitler's feats (in the 1930s) were something Britons could admire. For this comprehension can be a matter of cold calculation. The more one knows of "the opposite point of view," the "less puzzling" it is to clarify motives and "to know what to do" (*SWW*, III, 581). Botha and Smuts were statesmen because able to "see the other side's point of view" (*ItB*, 285).

To identify with others prevents one also from relapsing into savagery. Though Churchill was in many ways bellicose, he paradoxically brought a refined attitude to combat. In his first book, he declared, "Never despise your enemy is an old lesson, but it has to be learned afresh, year after year, by every nation" (*MFF*, 218), and in his maiden speech he made the courageous and wise remark, "If I were a Boer, I hope I should be fighting in the field." Whether dealing with a fellow Briton or a foreigner, he forwarded a seemingly contradictory policy of "force and generosity" (*MEL*, 366). Early he said, in a remark which adumbrates his theme of magnanimity in war, "All men improve under a generous treatment"; revenge is not a "dignified emotion for a great people to display" (*RW*, I, 412; II, 393). Marlborough's career was notably "free from the tiresome, baulking shadows of revenge" (*M*, II, 1029), which is "the most costly and long drawn out" (*EU*, 439) satisfaction, even as generosity "ranks among the noblest impulses" (*ItB*, 285).

Just as sympathetic identification with those in high office is most likely to be found in men holding, or aspiring to hold, leadership positions, so also is generosity a virtue that can be practiced only by those in positions of power, those able, if they wish, to punish, extort, persecute. And, if one trait marks Churchill's writings it is his (amoral, to some) celebration of power—not, he claimed, for the sake of self-aggrandisement, pomp, or domination of others, but in order to achieve things. His only novel, *Savrola*, is in good part a study of power, its roots, and its precariousness. In various works, he spoke, with reference to Randolph, Lloyd George, Marlborough, or himself, of the joy of being able to organize, plan, implement, of using the "desirable gift" of "giving orders" (*GC*, 218) and of having able men working for one. Though the goal was ultimately something noble like achieving lasting peace, high office was the means; an idea not embodied in legislative, administrative, or diplomatic form was hardly an idea for him. The exercise of power was itself therefore noble, notwithstanding the contrary views of idealists and purists. Few great men, he assures us in a sentence in *Savrola* which conjures up the personal diplomacy of World War II, lack a "charm of manner" (*S*, 147). Leaders may be unscrupulous but they try, as he claimed Marlborough did, to put national interests first or, as he hoped in the 1930s Hitler would, to "put away a discreditable past" (*SbS*, 53).

Conscious of possessing this voracious appetite, the skills which justify it, and the knowledge of what orders to give in a crisis, the Churchillian hero happily accepts difficult tasks. Even from so high a position as number two or three man, initiation of policy, as Churchill eloquently documented in the *World Crisis* and the *Second World War* from personal experience, is hindered by protocol or by consideration of the minds and egos of the superior. To become prime minister at a dangerous juncture (or for Marlborough to be freed in Germany of his Dutch allies and advisers) meant that at last one could "give directions over the whole scene" (*SWW*, I, 667). Power is a blessing for the man who knows in a crisis exactly

what order to give. "At the top there are great simplifica-
tions. . . . I was sure I should not fail" (*SWW*, II, 15; I, 667).

Power must, to be sure, be substantive and not shadowy.
Churchill often condemned the bearing of the pain of responsibility without the opportunity of taking effective action. He
spoke early of the "contemptible spectacle" (*PR*, 42) of a
minister in such a quandary, and after World War II he would
not undertake to solve problems "without the power to act by
deeds and not by words" (*StT*, 83). The achievement of high
office, moreover, is by itself no guarantee of success. Power
must be brought to bear on the body politic and on the world.
All large transactions, like war, require a "proper organization
at the summit which extends its control in all necessary directions" (*SbS*, 23). Churchill scorned the the World War I system
of a war cabinet free of departmental duties; lest there be
delay and paralysis, the key ministers had to direct the government. At the inception of World War II the "negative principle" was at first again too powerful in the British warmaking
machine, this time because committees multiplied "like rab-
bits." In order to function in a crisis, government also needed—as he thought Marlborough's experience likewise prove-
d—a national coalition. But this could not mean full repre-
sentation and consultation, for "action to be successful must
rest in the fewest number of hands possible" (*EoB*,
36)—preferably very few: Marlborough and Godolphin; Lloyd
George and Churchill; or just Churchill alone. "At the summit
there should be one mind playing over the whole field, faith-
fully aided and corrected, but not divided in its integrity"
(*SWW*, IV, 91). The person thus eminently situated should,
however, frequently confer in person with the leaders of other
nations.

With his propensity for seeing a crisis everywhere, Churchill usually wanted to retain coalitions and thought it a shame
that the parties should resume attacking each other at the end
of wars. He never had a very sanguine view of the party system or of elections. He understood leadership to be achieved
and exercised in a democratic context, of course; power obtained by violent deeds is "shabby recompense" for "shedding blood."[2] But for all of his worship of British democracy, a
refrain in his writings is that electioneering itself, by keeping

a country seething and vitiating commerce, is repulsive. "We all know what happens at elections" (*WES*, 24). Postwar elections in 1919 raised party issues in the crudest form and "cheapened" the nation; the World War II alliance with the United States was put under strain during an American presidential election. He objected to government by the Gallup poll; "you want to take a long view" (*UA*, 298) rather than being influenced by events of the moment. "Political systems can be appraised by the test of whether their leading representatives are or are not capable of making decisions in great matters on their merits, in defiance of their own interests" (*WC*, V, 37, 317). Baldwin, with eye cocked on a general election, shockingly failed that test in 1935 on the defense question, and frequent elections throughout the early 1930s could not help Britain find a way out of her economic troubles; in fact, postponed solutions. Danby's "administration" of 1673, Churchill assures us, "gave effect to the will of the people more fully than is usually done as the result of popular elections" (*M*, I, 97). Often would he complain of statesmen—W. J. Bryan in the 1890s, Lloyd George in 1919, Leon Blum and F. D. Roosevelt in the 1930s—tainted by election-time compromises against their better sense, some taking the "easy course in finance and social legislation" (*SbS*, 120).

Electioneering is merely one of the many headaches that are the obverse of the joy of holding power. Prominent position seems more attractive than it in fact is, for, as a weary, overworked dictator (Molara) represses the desire to send his secretary and official papers to hell, Churchill comments ironically: "Thus it is that great men enjoy the power they risk their lives to gain and often meet their deaths to hold" (*S*, 98). In war memoirs or *History*, Churchill remarks on the limits of power and glory, the mockery of high command, the illusory "pomp of power," and the terrible dilemmas which many leaders confront.

Worst of all is the fickleness of the monarch, the electorate, or Fortune. Young Churchill presents the hero of his novel, Savrola, and the hero of his biography, Randolph, in a predicament which he would in middle age delineate in the careers of Clemenceau, Lloyd George, himself, Marlborough, Chatham, and, in old age, most painfully in himself again: men whose services as counselors or leaders were much needed fallen from favor because of the blind working of the party system or the "fickle, ungrateful" populace. He being often under the sway of the "great man" theory of history, Churchill's recurrent and rather naive belief is that these men (and the assassinated Lincoln) could have brought a better world into being had they remained in power. Since even the most admired politician in a democracy can abruptly crash down in defeat, the tale which great men in high office have to tell is therefore tragic.

## II  *War*

These topoi interweave. That each man has his own tale should cause us to listen to and sympathize with those in power and, in turn, to practice magnanimity rather than revenge toward defeated adversaries. Since such wisdom and forbearance are rare, it behooves men who have them to reach the pinnacle of political power. Doing so in a legal, decent, and democratic fashion is, however, difficult in an open society, where a Gresham's law of ideas and rhetoric operates and where the great man is inevitably removed in mid-career.

Another set of recurring themes has to do with the uses of power in peace and war. Given Churchill's interests and experiences—congruent with the twentieth-century experience—these themes proved to be mainly principles of war. Not that Churchill continuously relished hostilities; on the contrary, he saw himself as adhering to a policy of avoiding war, a policy unpopular because few politicians or voters understood the unsentimental, even depraved, nature of men and nations.

However he might praise and practice magnanimity in the wake of victory, he was, before and during a fight, belligerent, almost savage. Whether in his conservative or liberal phases,[3] his writings contain a tough-mindedness which brought him into conflict with those he regarded as sentimental and therefore wrong—Little Englanders (antiimperialists), liberals, socialists, intellectuals, pacifists. Frankly imperialistic at first, he attacked in the 1890s "certain people in England" who were content to leave the Indian frontier tribes in their "state of degraded barbarism," some "idealists" even ascribing non-existent "family virtues to primitive peoples." Liberal

governments had "soothed" such souls by "disclaiming any
further acquisition of territory" (*MFF*, 129, 9, 31). This pacific
policy, perceived as a sign of weakness, merely incited the
natives to perfidy and rebellion. Eventually the British Army
would have to carry the war home to them in order to bring
hostilities to an end. Chuchill disliked the resultant cycle: was
this "always to be our method of war and conquest," from follies and withdrawal to "a great army striking an overwhelming
blow" (*RW*, II, 48)?

In the 1930s, though the problem was confronting not frontier tribes but European dictators, the issues remained the
same. The British government catered to pacifists, and at international conferences everyone praised disarmament plans,
"which spread out hope and soothing syrup," but killed them
quietly in committee. Because of this discrepancy between
the sentimental rhetoric of governments and the hard realities,
he often praised the idea of secret sessions of Parliament in
wartime and secret negotiations. He also rejected the pacifist
stance "that whatever foreign nations may do to us, under no
circumstances should we ever do anything to them. I will see
what they do first" (*FFT*, 86). China was a cautionary example;
it suffered from malice and oppression because of the "base
and perverted" (*SbS*, 138) pacifism ingrained in its people for
millenia. His classic statement of the problem as it existed in
the 1930s has since been applied by others to all sorts of situations, not always with great care for accuracy or relevance:
"Whereas 'appeasement' only encouraged their aggression
and gave the Dictators more power with their own peoples,
any sign of a positive counter-offensive by the Western Democracies immediately produced an abatement of tension"
(*SWW*, I, 248).

This toughmindedness was meant to avoid war. Yet, periodically, malicious foreign leaders arose at the same time as the
reins of British governments were in the hands of men too sentimental or vote-conscious to be toughminded. As a result, war
could not be avoided. Churchill brought to war not only an
appreciation of technology and a study of military science but
also that love of combat and of adversity which manifested itself in his politics. The idiosyncratic assertions in his first
books that some men are as exalted by ruin as others by victory
or that London should be defended to the bitter end proved

eerily true of himself in 1940. He often celebrated as the sovereign virtue in war the willingness to fight on though all hope was lost and once undertook a modest philosophical inquiry into the motives, noble and ignoble, which "induce men" to defy dangers. The Germans were excluded from his pantheon in part because they "do not always find the resources to confront approaching disaster, once their reason tells them that it is inevitable" (*OtV*, 154). So fascinated was he with gallant failures that in middle age he wrote a curious but typical essay, "Great Fighters in Lost Causes."[4]

### III  *History*

A third set of topoi deals with Churchill's vision of history. No detached, scholarly surveyor of the human enterprise, Churchill cannot be expected to provide a complex, comprehensive hypothesis as to the meaning of events. Such generalizations as he hazards arise from the concerns and occurrences of the moment, not from methodical ratiocination. And many, naturally, have to do with wars.

All great wars, he insisted, "have been won by superior will power wresting victory in the teeth of odds or upon the narrowest of margins" (*SSS*, 45). Certainly he thought that World War II was, like Waterloo and World War I, a "damned close run thing." When all dues had been paid to British courage and the like, "the House will not fail to discern the agate points upon which this vast improvement has turned. By what a small margin and by what strokes of fortune" (*EoB*, 25). History is filled with such fortunate turns. The American Republic was established a week before the French Revolution; "the flimsy, untested fabric of American unity and order had been erected only just in time" (*HESP*, III, 213). Or the American declaration of war on Britain was followed in a week by Napoleon's invasion of Russia. The pattern was repeated in 1917 when the fall of the czar was followed within weeks by the American entry into World War I.

The workings of the fortuitous were not confined to war. If in his first books Churchill noted how pervasive was the role of luck on the battlefield and in the military career, how easily years of work and heroism could be cut down by a stray bullet, in *Randolph Churchill* he traced the hardly less dramatic and

visible workings of chance in politics, and after World War I
he saw its workings in every aspect of life. Deeply conscious
of the role of chance in life, he often quoted from Kipling's
"If" the lines on triumph and disaster as impostors.

Luck makes itself felt as early as in the period of character
formation. We do not know what makes us do things, and
"small people, casual remarks, and little things very often
shape our lives more powerfully than the deliberate, solemn
advice of great people at critical moments" (*ATS*, 51). The unexpected turns in history show "how vainly man strives to control his fate"; in his major and minor works, Churchill expressed wonderment at the way a man's "greatest neglects or
failures may bring him good [and] even his greatest achievements may work him ill" (*M*, II, 142).

The same paradox, when applied to mankind itself, threw
into question the idea of progress. For if chance was so powerful, the advances wrought by modern science and democracy
remained precarious. All deliberate steps for improving the lot
of man, all attempts to impose design and order on the universe, were likely to fail or at least be deflected. Despite
numerous and confident extrapolations from the present (not a
few made by Churchill himself), the future was unpredictable
and the destiny of man uncertain.

Churchill's position on the basic modern belief in progress
accordingly changed. He grew up during the late Victorian
period, when the consensus was that the cessation of major
European wars, like the advance of technology in the West
and of western values in Asia and Africa, signaled the arrival of
a better age. In his early books, with their naive if not unques-
tioning praise of the imperial mission, he subscribed to the
belief in progress. Despite cycles and ironies, history is not
shapeless. Though great movements degenerate, "decay gives
birth to fresh life," regeneration goes on amid the garbage of
old systems. "The rise and fall of men and their movements
are only the changing foliage of the evergrowing tree of life,
while underneath a greater evolution goes on continually"
(*RW*, I, 58). To this extent was young Churchill a Victorian
optimist.

In books and speeches of his "radical" phase he seemed
committed to a belief in at least social progress. Beyond the
"distant mountains," he frequently sang in his speeches and

writings, "is the promise of the sun" (*LSP*, 210). The advent and aftermath of World War I, however, made that belief less tenable. The *World Crisis* reflects the general twentieth-century *angst*, and the writings of the 1930s and the 1940s juxtapose strictures on the horrors of modern life with nostalgic portraits of two better periods—the Age of Queen Anne, when life, despite or because of the absence of the dubious blessings of technology, seemed better; the Age of Queen Victoria, when the recent advent of technology stimulated the pleasing belief in progress and when the full consequences of the new ways had not yet become apparent. Ignoring nineteenth-century European atrocities in Africa and Asia, Churchill expressed fears that it would be long before men regained the Victorian belief that all men are necessary to one another. In politics and warmaking, moreover, great men were no longer in evidence as abundantly as heretofore.[5] With the disappearance of the old monarchies and aristocracies which fought each other according to a code, the "race-conscious masses" now fight wars that are more ruthless than ever.

The blame for all this lies with the very science and democracy which are thought to have brought about progress. The basic modern problem is that progress has been confined to technology, that events have swollen to vast proportions, "while the stature and intellect of man remain unchanged." Hence man's sufferings increase "under systems of mechanical barbarism and organized terror. . . . The most deadly instruments of war science have been joined to the extreme refinements of treachery and ruthlessness" (*US*, 52, 175, 231). Though prosperity by means of science is now within reach, only disasters have accumulated. The most advanced societies see a decline in personal preeminence, and the nineteenth-century parliamentary systems have everywhere in Europe been replaced by dictatorships, some of which threaten to return all Europeans to the Stone Age. Greater civility has meant greater pain, because "in the Stone Age the numbers were fewer, and the primitive creatures, little removed from animal origin, knew no better. We suffer more, and we feel more" (*Vi*, 84). History seems out of control; "the past no longer enables us even dimly to measure the future" (*ATS*, 272). Gone is the illusion of progress. And with it goes any theory of history that Churchill has the intellectual resources to entertain.

## CHAPTER 4

# *"Tales of Muddle": The Art of War*

### I  *At War With Experts*

CERTAINLY there was no progress in the art—as against the technology—of warmaking. That perception sometimes threatened to become Churchill's only theme. As a lifelong warrior—sometimes hot, sometimes cold, sometimes professional, sometimes amateur—as a participant in numerous military clashes, including two cataclysmic world wars, and as one who believed that history is simply "past politics and wars" ("drums and trumpet"), Churchill meditated long and hard on military matters and on how wars should be conducted. Most of his books are on war, and the same military issues have a way of recurring in his writings. Thus in the early *Savrola* and *Randolph Churchill* he took note of the idea of a fleet forcing its way through the Dardanelles; having burned his fingers with such an actual attempt in World War I, he recurred in the *History* and the *Second World War* to the question of ships against land fortresses and torpedoes and, by way of continuing his critique of the overly cautious admirals of the earlier world war, gave the advantage to the ships.

His iconoclasm and impatience no less than his brilliance quickly brought him into conflict with the military establishment. Judging from the numerous mistakes made by generals, Churchill early developed a profound distrust of experts, especially the military sort. He speaks of a "rugged ridge, made famous by the blundering collision of two armies, worthless except for the tactical purpose of the moment and probably ill-adapted and wrongly selected even for that" (*RC*, II, 49).

One problem is that "all professional opinion is conservative." It took a year of World War I before the helmet was adopted in the face of high-placed scorn and a high casualty rate.[1] The generals were merely being true to the tradition which had opposed the introduction of steam, ironclad ships, propellers, and submarines into the navy and of locomotives, pistols, tanks, and warplanes into the army. Churchill's military teachers at Sandhurst were, as he described them, typical in being completely deluded as to what the next century would bring. Most generals lack imagination. (He often privately called them "dug out trash," "mediocrities," "boobies," "tyrants.") Products of routine and inflexibility, resembling experts of any sort, they have little in common with heroes like Marlborough and Napoleon. Lifelong study makes for rigidity, and the maxims of leading generals, which were passing observations on living facts, are treated blindly as the laws of nature. The rules of war, though simple on paper, were worked out by genius, which cannot be acquired by reading or routine. Since such special talent is rare and since in modern war nearly everything changes from year to year, "most wars are mainly tales of muddle" (*M*, I, 569) and "catalogues of blunders" (*SWW*, III, 353).

Another problem is that the frailty of the military experts cannot be readily perceived or acted upon by the politicians, and Churchill's ire is aimed at the War Office as well. In the Boer War, the British Army was quickly shown to be unready for the challenge. Its general was a sedentary, unintelligent man who "plodded on from blunder to blunder and from one disaster to another, without losing either the regard of his country or the trust of his troops, to whose feeding as well as his own he paid serious attention" (*MEL*, 234). Even when the War Office does set about assessing the generals, it is likely to use the wrong guidelines. The civilians do not realize that combat is a gamble, that generals cannot be expected to fight without losses. To place undue emphasis on the loss of guns or ships is to restrain the pugnacity of the fighting men. In the Boer War, moreover, "All the generals had received the most severe warnings against incurring casualties. Frontal attacks were virtually prohibited. Everything was to be done by kindness and manœuvre: instructions admirable in theory, paralyzing in effect!" (*MEL*, 338). Generals should be judged rather by their ideas and effort than by their successes or casualty rates.

In his earliest books, Churchill adopted a tone of humility and self-deprecation but went on to note that expert opinion is "based on partial information and warped by local circum-stances" (*MFF*, 298); the experts had said that the building of the desert railway (in the Sudan War) was impossible, or they had been caught by surprise by the revolts of Indian tribes-men and South African settlers. Noting how artillery officers said that certain guns could not be brought to the top of a hill, while a naval lieutenant was confident of success, he con-cludes gleefully, as he would in World War II, "The contrast in spirit was very refreshing" (*LLP*, 309). Half a century later, citing Gladstone's saying, "Expert knowledge is limited knowledge," Churchill noted that several severe errors in the Admiralty had been "strongly supported by professional opin-ion on the highest and most disinterested grounds" (*EU*, 267).

In the *River War*, although awed by the coolness with which Kitchener, against expert advice, made modern technology seal the doom of the foe, Churchill begins his lifelong criti-cism of individual generals. Kitchener's tactics, his handling of various artillery bombardments, of the wounded, of cavalry forces at Omdurman (including that famous charge of the 21st Lancers), his "rash and over-confident" running of "unneces-sary dangers" (*RW*, II, 272), his political error of profaning the Mahdi's tomb—all are explicitly censured. In the books on the Boer War, a war which Churchill elsewhere calls the grave of so many British military reputations, the numerous failings of General Redvers Bullers, to be revealed a generation later in Churchill's autobiography, are suppressed. The portrait he draws in the novel *Savrola* of the military mind suggests that Churchill enjoyed army life *despite* the presence of his fellow and superior officers. An admiral is ready for civil war because "I have had my big gun trained on the Parliament House for the last month, and I mean to let it off one day" (*S*, 96), while a major is eager to fire on a crowd because "it will enable me to conclude these experiments in penetration, which we have been trying with soft-nosed bullet. A very valuable experi-ment, Sir" (*S*, 11). Men like the admiral, who "live their lives in great machines, become involved in the mechanism them-selves." The admiral "neither knew nor cared for anything" other than ships; even if the target were freedom fighters or his native town, "as long as the authority to fire reached him through the proper channel, he was content; after that, he re-garded the question from a purely technical standpoint" (*S*,

96). Another officer "was one of those who fear little but independent responsibility; now that he had a leader, he followed and obeyed with military precision" (*S*, 138).

During and after World War I, the changed nature of warfare as well as the quality of the generals involved in that conflict heightened Churchill's contempt. Since Britain had not fought a major war in a long time, since men always "rely upon the weapons and lessons of a by-gone war" (*WC*, V, 290), and since the progress of military technology had been greatly accelerated, the military services had much to learn from novel experiences and situations. The admirals eventually learned their lesson all too well—that is, not well at all—for overestimation of the new weapons made them altogether battle shy. They remained content with having wrested mastery of the sea and penned in the German fleet. Against the reigning Admiralty view that war was the business of the army and that the navy performed in an ancillary capacity only, Churchill asserted that "the Navy was a gigantic instrument of offensive war" (*WC*, II, 541), but he could not, he records, prod Britain's supreme weapon into playing its proper role. The Near Eastern campaign, for instance, was bogged down in costly and laborious advances through the desert. Utilizing the navy for the "obvious maneuver of landing an army behind the Turks" (*WC*, IV, 44) would have severed the foe's communications and ended the war there at a stroke.

Admiral Jellicoe, in particular, allowed the German fleet to slip out of his grasp in the Jutland encounter because of a series of blunders caused mainly by rigid adherence to a preconceived system. All the troubles Churchill had taken at the Admiralty to construct at huge expense the superdreadnoughts, with superlative speed, guns, armor, had been for just such situations. But the admirals, instead of exploiting their speed, allowed these ships to trail the fleet. Part of the trouble was due to the training which the naval officers received. Churchill was surprised to find that they were never required to read about naval history. They were captains of ships, not of war; specialists without a larger view. Such conservatism and blindness was even more painfully in evidence in the army. Military training encourages conformity rather than independence of mind, ability to think, talk, write, or individual exertion.

The most "monstrous" convention which the public mind and the press accepted, he lamented, was that generals and admirals were "more competent to deal with the broad issues of war than abler men in other spheres of life" (*WC*, III, 249). Heavy was the price paid at Gallipoli and elsewhere by "the Admirals who thought only of the Grand Fleet and the Generals who thought only of the Main Army" (*WC*, II, 539). The generals were far "out of touch with reality." It took the high command "nearly two years and every conceivable mistake" to learn to use the tank in the proper manner. Fortunately the German general staff was no better. "In truth these high military experts all belong to the same school," all have that "peculiar professional note" which traps them in "the rut of traditional and conventional methods" (*WC*, II, 81-82, 502; III, 187; IV, 60-61, 118).

Churchill is especially vitriolic on the supreme commanders of each nation. He depicts Joffre as a placid, unfeeling vegetable living in comfort and serene routine, knowing only offensives, committing error upon error, and, on the basis of stultified strategy and administration, sending entire armies "into the blue." The 1915 offensives under Joffre lost 1,300,000 men for 500,000 Germans. It was not until 1918 that the Germans began to lose more—under Ludendorff's offensives. "It was their own offensive, not ours that consummated their ruin. They were worn down not by Joffre, Nivelle, and Haig, but by Ludendorff" (*WC*, III, 45). On the German side, Falkenhayn, another creature of convention, was equally unaffected by the 1914 disasters in the West and the 1915 victories in the East. The Austrian commander, Von Hötzendorf, ignored the power of the defensive, underrated the Russians, and through impatience nearly destroyed the Austrian armies at once. "The school of formula had vanquished the school of fact, the professional bent of mind had overriden the practical; submission to theory had replaced the quest for reality" (*WC*, III, 70, 73). The German defeat can in part be attributed to this lack of vision. Churchill cites, among other causes, two premature exposures (of the U-boat and gas weapons, both in 1915) and two errors of military strategy (attacking West and East simultaneously and using resources for a desperate offensive in 1918 rather than for building an impregnable defense line on the Rhine or Meuse). Even in the relatively minor post-

World War I Irish crisis, the British generals contributed "unhelpful counsel," demanding universal martial law in Ireland: "How this would have solved the problem was never explained.... I never received during my tenure of the War Office any practical or useful advice on this subject from these quarters" (*WC*, V, 301).

Years later, in the *History,* U. S. Grant joins the gallery of prominent generals for whom Churchill has little respect. His "brutal and simple" plan was "summed up in the word 'Attrition.' " When the Union suffered twice the battle losses of the Confederacy, an undeterred Grant repeated his strategy. His "unflinching butchery" was ended by the result of one battle—seven thousand casualties in an hour and the refusal of the survivors to renew the assault. Surely "more is expected of the high command than determination in thrusting men to their doom." Grant's "performances," although a "deadly form of war" which eventually "gained their purpose" (*HESP*, IV, 193-96), must be regarded as the negation of generalship. Grant was clearly a World War I-type general whose obsession with the head-on offensive and war of attrition led to slaughter rather than advance. The man he had replaced, McClellan, failed in different ways: "To make sure of not running undue risks"—like certain of Churchill's World War I admirals and World War II generals—"he lost a day and failed to win the battle." He erred also in fighting the battle from his headquarters; unlike Jackson, Lee, Marlborough, Frederick, Napoleon, "he made his dispositions and left the battle to fight for itself" (*HESP*, IV, 163).

In the *Second World War,* Churchill takes mischievous delight in showing himself the peer of his military advisers. They were hardly perfect; none had pointed out the weakness of the British defenses in France and Belgium, and, after having underrated the blitz, they overrated it. They were wrong on the dangers of invasion of Britain in 1941, on Hitler's alleged imminent victory in Russia in 1942, on the alleged fall of Germany in 1944, on attacking Sardinia rather than Sicily. Intelligence estimates of enemy capacity proved to be exaggerated and thereby a "deterrent upon action" (*SWW*, III, 767). Nor did the German general staff "always forecast events with unerring accuracy" (*SWW*, IV, 13), as their timidity in 1936-1938 and, later, the survival of Britain and Russia proved. "I only mention this to show that even the most expert professional opinion may sometimes err amid the many uncertainties of war" (*SWW*, III, 422).

One of his running quarrels with the services, especially the army, was over the sheer inertia and inefficiency of their "horribly bloated" bureaucracies. All commanders unduly magnify the difficulties, ask "for everything they can think of, and always represent their own forces at a minimum" (*SWW*, III, 513). The army bureaucratic mind proved an obstacle in other ways. The modern innovation of commando or storm troops aroused the suspicion and prejudices of the army establishment. In an age of rapidly changing methods of warfare, the professional soldier's distaste for novel devices was dangerous. Related obstacles were snobbery, which withheld promotion from men of the wrong class, and the inbred seniority system, which withheld it from men of extraordinary ability or independent manner.

Perhaps the biggest obstacle Churchill faced in the military establishment in World War II was the defensive state of mind, the mental prostration before the will of the enemy because of memories of World War I slaughters (caused by obsession with mindless offensives) and the tendency to prepare for the last war. He had, he recalls, to scotch ideas of abandoning the Eastern Mediterranean and perhaps even Malta. The army insisted, for every operation, on its routine extravagant requirements and on exact dates, thus reducing flexibility and daring. The officers of the three services, moreover, by presenting the sum of their fears and of the difficulties in each service, paralyzed all action. This cautiousness contrasted with the reckless gambling, calculation, and vigor of the Germans. If only those attempts with overwhelming chance of success were to be made, he concludes, a complete defensive posture would be the outcome, for certainties are rare in war, and trying to be safe everywhere is a fallacy. Delay merely increases risks and difficulties; the natural inclination to prudence and caution is self-defeating.

Churchill carefully catalogs what he takes to be the failures of his generals—in critiques which are, of course, one-sided and disputed by military historians. Wavell, in charge of the only sizeable army Britain had in the field in the first years of the war, dispersed his forces, made slow use of supplies painfully shipped to him at the height of the blitz, ignored Churchill's demands for amphibious operations in Lybia, sided with the nervous admirals on not sending supply convoys through the Mediterranean, neglected the defenses of Crete, chose the wrong field commanders, and moved too slowly in Central Africa, into Greece and Iraq, and against the daring Rommel. Replacing him with Auchinleck, who had, by contrast, nimbly pacified Iraq, Churchill soon found himself, as he thought, facing the same difficulties. The new commander feared to act concurrently in the desert and Syria, sent the best British troops to quiet Cyprus, often postponed offensive action in quest of a "set-piece battle" and a two to one superiority over the Germans, chose field commanders unwisely, defended Tobruk supinely, so lacked initiative as to have to be ordered into the offensive and, when at last attacking, sent home optimistic dispatches which revealed a lack of comprehension of the military situation. His decision to retreat to Egypt was the final straw.

Not only did the Middle East Command remain a troublesome place after the replacement of Wavell with Auchinleck, but Wavell's being shifted to India merely brought the troubles to Asia when Japan attacked: a badly thought-out campaign in Malaya; the neglect of Singapore's landward defenses; the crumbling of Allied positions throughout the East Indies; and a Burma campaign going "from bad to worse," as the "fatal lassitude of the Orient" stole "over all these commanders" (*SWW*, IV, 935). Despite his reverent treatment of Generals Alexander and Montgomery, the refrain of his memoirs is that, decades after his entry onto the world stage, Britain was still plagued by epigones—at least to hear Churchill tell it—of Kitchener and Bullers and Joffre et al.

## II  *Some Military Principles*

Churchill brought to his various posts definite ideas for change. These were based on his "military training and study of the art of war, and the maxims of the great captains of the past,"[2] precisely the sort of study he thought the military experts lacked. On the strength of that, he had the confidence—and the temerity—to argue with generals on their own ground and to presume to teach them some basic principles of warmaking.

For one thing, he kept his eye on the problems and challenges peculiar to each war, the topographical, technological, logistical conditions of combat. In his early writings he noted the worthiness and mobility of the foes (guerillas in Cuba, India, South Africa) and their exploitation of their native hilly locale. In the Boer War and World War I he observed how modern rifle, machine gun, and artillery fire made frontal attacks prohibitive and rendered, as the military establishment did not at once see, the sword and horse obsolete. In the *River War,* he also first remarked on how difficult in modern war it becomes to send out a force without addressing complex logistical problems and the vested interests of the various army departments, problems he recurred to in the *World Crisis* and notably the *Second World War.*

Churchill's early emphasis on the importance of the new firepower and his contempt for the traditional lance and sword were to be vindicated by subsequent wars. He was a keen prophet in other ways as well. In a footnote to a discussion of the plague, he suggests that "some day science may call the mighty bacillus into the dispute of nations" (*LLP,* 142). He suspects that in future wars troops will no longer "be handled in masses" but "in widely dispersed formations where they will have to think for themselves"—radio partly falsified that prediction—"and with regard to artillery, it appears that the advantages of defensive action, range, concealment, and individual initiative may easily counterbalance numbers and discipline" (*LLP,* 420, 444). Pursuit may become impossible. "A hundred bold men with magazine rifles on a ridge can delay the whole army" (*LLP,* 455). The latter indeed became a serious problem in World War I, but the greater dispersal he speaks of here was not adopted until World War II (when the advent of the plane caused him at first to think, only somewhat prematurely, that the day of large land battles was gone for good).

The salient fact about World War I was trench warfare and the consequent necessity of turning the flank by amphibious and overseas operations. In World War II there was the only slowly understood new interplay of armor, air, and sea power. Such technological changes which at first resulted in stalemates and in a reversion to defensive postures should not cause men to lose sight of aggressiveness; "in war armies must

fight" (*SWW*, III, 5). They merely required ingenuity and resourcefulness. Conventional aggressiveness could not be sub-
stituted for planning, especially in a modern war, with its use
of elaborate technical apparatus. The Germans knew that. The
blitzkrieg, as first exhibited in Poland, consisted of a spear-
point mass of fast-moving armored vehicles which broke down
the defenses by rendering artillery, perhaps for the first time
since the invention of gunpowder, impotent and which advanced an unprecedented hundred miles a day. A further development of German military science was the fusion of air
and land forces. The invasion of Crete was the first massed
airborne attack in history. As air power and mechanized troops
replaced masses of men and high ammunition expenditure in
importance, natural obstacles like the Dutch canals, Ardennes
forest, or even the English Channel, were suddenly of little
account, and the Maginot Line was easily circumvented.

The World War I military experts' obliviousness to the significance of the helmet, the Stokes gun, the warplane, and the
tank was, Churchill thought, symptomatic of their ignorance of
a basic fact of warmaking—that throughout history the balance
between East and West depended on a knowledge of arms.
That is why in World War I, when a general said that Britons
must put their backs into the war, Churchill added, "We must
do more. We must put our brains into it."[3] And he acted accordingly. He later boasted that in this war of "mechanics and
brains," the Admiralty was "in hot pursuit of most of the great
key inventions and ideas of the war; and this long in advance
of every other nation, friend or foe" (*WC*, II, 399). He is notably proud of having dabbled in the tank, a matter "not in any
way my business and in regard to which I had not received
expert advice in any responsible military quarter" (*WC*, II,
69). It was a perennial problem. Years later, Churchill reminded people of how the tank, which revolutionized war,
was forced on the War Office by outsiders, who "would have
just as hard work today to force a new idea on it" (*WES*, 328).

He flourishes in the *World Crisis* a March, 1918, memo
sketching plans for the 1919 campaign. In it he urged the development of the new methods of warfare made possible by
the airplane, tank, gas, and machine gun. He envisaged 10,000
tanks moving on a front of four hundred kilometers followed
by infantry, behind which 10,000 caterpiller tractors would

carry supplies cross country and leave the roads free for artillery reserves. The *Second World War* is replete with his interest in what he called now the "Wizard War," with its unintelligible language, its numerous moves and countermoves, as
either or both sides raced ahead with research in sea and aerial
mines, sensitive fuses, radar, jet propulsion, rockets, snorkel
submarines, artificial harbors, nuclear bombs.

Another basic principle was that when attacked on two
fronts, one should concentrate everything on destroying the
main attacking force; "to try to be safe everywhere is to be
strong nowhere" (*SWW*, IV, 16). In World War I, he therefore
favored concentrating the fleet; if Britain won the big battle,
all else would fall into place. With the development of the
tank, as a result of his prodding, Churchill called for the careful harnessing of power in an army which was to be–in the
words of a favorite antithesis of his–"crouched" rather than
"sprawled," that is, with a large proportion in reserve and
training ("Strategic Reserve," "Army of Maneuver") rather
than wasted on offensives and which was given by tanks and
airplanes the "greatest possible lateral mobility" (*WC*, IV,
195). In the 1930s he noted that while Japan is "sprawled in
China," Russia is "crouched ready to spring in the North"
(*SbS*, 214). In 1940, he thought it important for Britain to have
what France lacked: a large central reserve of "mass of maneuver." This lack he held responsible for the fall of France
and, later, for the fall of Hitler. In the *History*, he answers
criticism of the Roman defense procedure–building a line of
eight fortresses along the English coast to protect four
hundred miles of coastlines–by conjecturing that the eight
were bases for a British-Roman fleet. This policy, similar to
that urged by Drake for meeting the Armada at sea, parallels
his own idea of a strong central reserve instead of an extensive
but thinned out defense line.

Principles have, however, their exceptions, and "forecasts
are usually falsified and preparations always in arrear" (*SWW*,
III, 657). The decisive theater can also be overstressed, for, as
"the battle draws everything into itself, there are moments
when gains of priceless value in other quarters can be
gathered cheaply" (*SWW*, V, 692). Hitler, concentrating on the
coming invasion of Russia, lost the chance to take a great prize,
Iraq, at little cost. Improvisation is as important as detailed

planning. Churchill is aware that no battle ever repeats itself, that success does not arise from following rules or models. None of the textbook maneuvers can work by themselves, for each battle depends on the interplay of many factors, which can be assayed only in the mind of one man "from hour to hour making subconsciously all the unweighable adjustments."

Churchill uses Marlborough's preference for improvisation and imaginative maneuvers rather than for set sieges as a critique of World War I generals, whose "dangerous prudence of conventional opinion prevented unexpected and so-called eccentric alternatives" (*M*, II, 425). The proper objects in war are, in any case, armies, not cities. In the American Revolution, the British forces were dispersed over five hundred miles and divided between locales. By contrast, in the American Civil War, Lee always sought the "decisive and final battle which he knew could alone save the Confederacy" (*HESP*, IV, 162). Lincoln understood this too, for when Lee moved north, Hooker's proposed march on Richmond was vetoed by the president on the ground that "not Richmond but Lee's army was his proper objective" (*HESP*, IV, 180).

In that war, indeed, Churchill for once found himself siding with a general. He admired Lee as "one of the noblest" (*HESP*, IV, 131) of all Americans and one of the greatest of all generals. But that same war dramatized the basic dilemma in military-civilian relations. If the generals are, as often is the case, imperfect and slow, they need to be prodded by the civilian leaders. To make audacious plans on paper and give a general directives to beat the enemy effects nothing; guidance and control are needed from above. Even if generals tend to consider all directions from civilian leaders as obstructions, their job is simply to prepare the best plans and leave the responsibility for the choice of operations to the civilian leader. Churchill's working hypothesis was that strategy and tactics are matters of common sense and that any imaginative civilian could solve problems in them and let the soldier translate the solution into military terms. (Hence his classic memorandum of 13 August 1911 on war strategy.) In the *Second World War*, he portrays himself as the custodian of what his local commanders ignored—the balancing of conflicting needs among the worldwide fronts of the empire.

Such license in the hands of the civilian leaders may prove,

however, to be counterproductive. As a rule, Churchill sometimes (not so consistently) remarks, generals should not be interfered with, and he justified the venerable naval policy of
not tampering with an admiral's dispositions by means of
modern wireless because the Admiralty rarely has sufficient
information and because such action would "destroy initiative" (SSS, 63). Even the great Lincoln, with his vacillation,
his inexperience in military affairs, his making appointments
on "purely political grounds," his yielding too readily to
clamor for change, is a "classic instance of the dangers"
(HESP, IV, 150) of civilian interference. Since Jefferson Davis
similarly interfered with Lee, Churchill conjectures that had
McClellan and Lee been free to fight as they wished, "the end
would have been the same, but the war would have been less
muddled, much shorter, and less bloody" (HESP, IV, 170). The
actions of Hooker and Grant, on the other hand, suggest that
some interference was desirable; hence, "no rule can be laid
down upon the High Command of states and armies in war. All
depends upon the facts and the men. But should a great general appear the civil government would be wise to give him
full scope at once in the military sphere" (HESP, IV, 201). Lee
was such a titan, yet he was not appointed commander in chief
until 1865.

Part of the problem with most generals was the "serious misfortunes" caused by the manner in which they rose in rank
merely by serving time or as a result of increases in the size of
the army. The military establishment does not reward brains.
Churchill doubted "whether the fact that a man has gained the
Victoria Cross for bravery as a young officer fitted him to
command an army twenty or thirty years later" (MEL, 303).
Promotion should go "for services and not for service" (S, 15);
and why could there not be any thirty-year-old generals if men
are at their peak at that age?

Another part of the problem is remoteness from the facts.
When studying Marlborough's battles, Churchill notes how in
military operations a general like Marlborough depended on
intimate knowledge of front-line conditions either through his
own presence or through young officers who knew his mind
and gave eyewitness reports. The great commander had to
have an "almost godlike" combination of mental, moral, and
physical qualities. His presence and demeanor were decisive.

Churchill himself tried to live up to that ideal. In the *Second World War*, because of his love of front-line visits, he relished becoming for a "short spell 'the man on the spot' " (*SWW*, IV, 456), instead of passively waiting for communiqués from far away. The World War I generals, by contrast, did not. Far from being battlefield heroes in the mold of Marlborough, they were men glued to their telephones, like "speculators with large holdings" when the stock market is falling. Even the once favored Ian Hamilton contributed to the Dardanelles debacle by keeping aloof, as, in different circumstances in World War II, did Auchinleck.

Such an absence was not an oversight but a failure of vision. Throughout his life, Churchill looked for the man of broad vision, who could see strategy in large terms. His youthful descriptions of Ian Hamilton, anticipating those of Foch, Marlborough, and Napoleon, contain a key Churchillian value (misapplied, as it turned out, to Hamilton): "His mind is built upon a big scale, capable of thinking in army corps and if necessary in continents" (*IH*, 135). The great generals of history won, in contrast with modern ones, by stratagem based on comprehensive vision, not by slaughter. They knew that true politics in war are true strategy. The Dardanelles expedition, for instance, was meant to bring the small Balkan states in on the Allied side. No antagonism exists between politics and strategy, but "between war motives and all other motives." War thought has a vital integrity and includes everything that makes victory possible—moral, political, economic. A policy is as real as a shell, and force has various manifestations.[4] Generals and politicians therefore had to overcome their natural tendency to compartmentalize and specialize.

To dissent from orthodox doctrine and adhere to a comprehensive global vision requires not only enlightenment but also a willingness to take chances. From the beginning does Churchill sound the theme of uncertainty in war and the consequent necessity of risk-taking. "Without the risk of defeat no victory can be won" (*LLP*, 368), nor war be made. At Pretoria, Roberts, "a general great enough to take all risks and overcome all dangers," advanced "without waiting for more supplies" in order to "profit by the enemy's disorder." He "played for a great stake," and because he won, men easily "forget the adverse chances" (*IH*, 297). Hence "armchair critics" should be tolerant of "men who try daring coups and fail" (*LLP*, 386). If the War Office evaluates officers pedantically, initiative will wither as generals "divide responsibility," ask "for orders and instructions," and fight "only on the limited liability principle" (*IH*, 28).

A basic difficulty in World War I was, he thought, excessive caution. Churchill reminded the British admirals that "absolute security means something very like absolute paralysis," that "hazard and uncertainty pervade all operations of war," and that dwelling on dangers may be a mask for simple fear: "War lies largely in the region of chance. Those who are committed to the 'No' principle may summon chance to their aid to multiply their difficulties and fortify their fears" (*WC*, I, 319, 412; II, 269, 276, 343). He insisted on the importance of prosecuting war in a forthright manner, of expecting and accepting the loss of artillery, ships, and men. The great commander does not "rest on the lessons of the past or prepare himself to repeat the triumphs of a former battle." He knows when to drop maxims and caution, unlike the general who always wished to look before he leaped. There are limits beyond which prudence and caution cease to contribute to the gaining of victory. By contrast, Eisenhower's decision to proceed with the Normandy invasion on June 6 in spite of meteorological uncertainties worked. He made many such correct decisions because "the natural bias that moved him" in such decisions "was very much more in favor of 'Aye' than of 'No' " (*Vi*, 201).

### III   *Napoleon – The Model of a Modern Major General*

Against this dismal record – consisting of both what he read about the military experts of the past and what he witnessed in his own long career, to wit, the flouting of commonsense principles by numberless generals – Churchill could set the example of a few great men. They were more than just generals. They were able to make peace as well as win the war. They saw the political problems as inextricable from the military ones. They were Carlylean shapers of history.

One of these great men was Cromwell, an ambitious, fanatic, "lightning-charged being," who receives more attention in the *History* than nearly anyone else and who forces an ambivalent Churchill into near self-contradiction. Astute, efficient, "avid for the power and command which he was sure he could wield" (*HESP*, II, 197), he was the only man combining "military command with an outstanding Parliamentary position." A "harsh, terrific," person on an erratic, opportunist, self-centered course, he experienced "well-meant puzzled plungings and surgings" (*HESP*, II, 212). Churchill loathes Cromwell's self-pitying rhetoric and the fanaticism which "invested his mission not only with a martial but a priestly aspect" (*HESP*, II, 223) and which turned cold-blooded, calculated massacre into a holy war with words like "righteousness" and "mercy." Sometimes Cromwell seems a hollow ambitious man, exploiting religious issues; sometimes, a sincere agonizing soul full of Christian humility.

Yet this enigmatic soul became the "champion of Protestantism, the arbiter of Europe, the patron of learning and the arts"; his "passion for England was as fervent as Chatham's. No one can remain unconscious of his desire to find a moral basis for his power," of his sense of duty to God and country. Nor was his dictatorship repressive in the modern fashion. Invoking light and reason rather than force, dreaming of a "union and a right understanding embracing Jews and Gentiles," saving the cause of Parliament, withstanding the ambition of his generals, he "cannot be wholly barred from his place in the forward march of liberal ideas." He truly protected the old England "against the terrible weapon he and Parliament had forged. Without Cromwell there might have been no advance, collapse, recovery." Amid the ruins of an old society, he "towered up, the sole agency by which time could be gained for healing and regrowth." So full of admiration, in spite of himself, is Churchill for this successful warrior-statesman-diplomat that the dismissal or rejection, if it be that, seems to come painfully: Cromwell also stands, unfortunately, for the dictatorship and military rule which "is in lasting discord with the genius of the English race" (*HESP*, II, 242-44).

Another titan was Churchill's own ancestor, the duke of Marlborough, whose strategy of mobility, artifice, and surprise required the craft of executing movements of extraordinary rapidity, brilliance of mind, a sure instinct, high troop morale, and resulted in a unique ten-year unbroken record of victories.[5]

Yet much as he revered his ancestor, Churchill was even

more obsessed by Napoleon. He read much on him and periodically dreamed of writing his biography; he even wanted his favorite performer, Charlie Chaplin, to play the Corsican in a serious role in a silent film for which Churchill would write the script. References to Napoleon abound in his works as to no other personage, not even Marlborough. He regarded Napoleon as a supreme genius. This worship, like the respect for Hitler expressed in the 1930s, is a case of Churchill's love of proficiency triumphing over his patriotism, of the amoral perspective triumphing over his tendency to moralize, of his activism and animal love of war triumphing over his basically decent instincts. To many contemporaries, Churchill seemed dangerous, deranged, or hateful for seeing in himself, or trying too hard to be like, Napoleon (or Marlborough), and indeed the *Second World War* has several irrelevant but revealing, egocentric pages on how Eisenhower and George VI labored earnestly and long to dissuade Churchill from participating in the Normandy landings.

Napoleon belongs to that very small club of warriors-states-men-diplomats, the other five members of which are Alexander, Hannibal, Caesar, Marlborough, and Frederick the Great, who are for Churchill—to the revulsion of most modern readers—the summit of human creativity. (A man like Ludendorff is excluded from it on the grounds of knowing only military matters and nothing else; Napoleon, Churchill is sure, would have handled the German strategy of 1918 much better.)[6] As a man of action, Napoleon was comparable only to Julius Caesar (who was greater because magnanimous), and he brought a revival of Roman solidarity, a unification (much enviable in the 1930s) of Europe, albeit "under Gallic forms."

His was a name for Churchill to conjure with, a synonym for such concepts as range, precision, ambition, efficacy, superlativeness, all-around greatness. No one, Churchill declares at one point, "not even Napoleon himself" (*WES*, 300), would be able to discharge supreme power hedged with limitations. In the *World Crisis* Churchill speaks of the German victory as a military success on the Napoleonic scale. The Corsican is a point of reference or a touchstone: displeased with a general who made his troops run seven miles, Churchill asked, "Could Napoleon have run seven miles across country at Austerlitz?" (*SWW*, III, 730). To make us understand Lee's predicament at Gettysburg, he invokes the image of Napoleon at Waterloo. In a debate on a vote of confidence in 1942, he declared himself ready to step down and serve under anyone who had the requisite Napoleonic and Christian qualities, could such a one be found. That Napoleon towered over mere generals and experts is shown by the fact that "even the tactics of Napoleon's great victories have been shown over and over again to have been utterly foolish and puerile by the military critics" (*RW*, I, 457). This was a severe judgment on them, not on him. The reason is that a great general is more than just a leader of troops: he must, like the Corsican at Toulon (whose youth Churchill envied), understand "not only the military significance of the captured fort, but the whole set of moral and political forces upon which the Royalist defence hung" (*HESP*, III, 236).

Churchill spoke frequently of the "glories of the Napoleonic era" (*ItB*, 101), of Napoleon as "the most splendid of tyrants,"[7] of his campaign in 1809 as "among the finest examples of military genius" (*HESP*, III, 265). Though he also became a conqueror in the fashion of Alexander, casting his eye on the Orient, the Corsican spread the idealism and dynamism of the French Revolution, and his overthrow meant for Europe a relapse to reactionary authority and "Old World hierarchies." Yet even in defeat and death, he left a legacy of nationalism.

It is indeed curious that, though Marlborough was Churchill's ancestor, though Churchill had early read Macaulay and others on the duke, though he had been conscious of Marlborough's greatness and had expected—and was expected by others, including publishers with generous advances—some day to write a biography of him, Marlborough is much less referred to in Churchill's writings than is Napoleon. As early as the *River War*, the Corsican looms large as the supreme military genius, one whose authority is invoked on various technical military and diplomatic questions, such as the proportion of soldiers to be on the front lines. In the *World Crisis*, he is again the one figure who looms large: his sayings and insights; the battles he fought and the strategic moves he made famous; his impact on Russia, Britain, Germany; his policies and diplomacy. The thoughts and actions of European leaders are compared and contrasted with the Corsican: Joffre "was not Napoleon," and Falkenhayn was intimidated by the example of Napoleon.

In the biography of Marlborough, Napoleon is referred to even more than usual, and in the *Second World War,* he is yet once more by far the single most dominant historical figure. Though England's bitter foe, he is the greatest of generals; his obiter dicta are again sprinkled through the work, and his famous military strokes are referred to contemporary battles. He is also called to mind because of the many curious parallels with Hitler's career and wars.

Among Napoleon's sayings often quoted by Churchill is the complaint—noteworthy with reference to the stance Churchill takes in his world war memoirs—that his admirals think that "war can be made without running risks" (*RW*, II, 233). In the Boer War books, Churchill invokes Napoleon's famous *"toujours l'audace"* (*LLP*, 187). Elsewhere, in speaking of the correctness of Marlborough's search for an advantageous strategic position in which to fight the grand single battle (rather than waste time over sieges or over securing every inch of territory), Churchill adds, "the rest would follow, as Napoleon would say, *par surcroît"* (*M*, II, 225). Marlborough was roused from depression "to the mood of Napoleon before Wagram; *'La bataille répondra' "* (*M*, II, 328).

Other common Napoleonic ideas are that war should be made to support war and that constitutions should be short and obscure. The Corsican also lurks behind some of Churchill's original-sounding sentences: if he had said that God is on the side with the heaviest artillery, his admirer said that the Allies (in World War II) "walk in fear of the Lord" albeit also "very heavily armed" (*OtV*, 21) or that the Kerensky government would have survived if it had had the "blessing of Providence and a rather better telephone service" (*GC*, 107). Nor does Napoleon speak to Churchill by words alone; Churchill cites the Corsican's feats as proof that rivers are never a secure shield before advancing armies or that without meddling unnecessarily a great general can yet think things through to the last detail.

Rather as sports fans do with their favorite stars, Churchill periodically compares and contrasts his heroes. As the "glittering adventurer of the eighteenth century," Napoleon differs from the "puzzled, self-questioning, but explosive spirit" of the seventeenth century, Cromwell. The Corsican, without all scruples, was "sure of himself" and his desire for supreme power in the world, while Cromwell, "crafty and ruthless," yet always a "reluctant and apologetic dictator, deplored the arbitrary character of his own rule, but had no difficulty in persuading himself that his authority sprang from both Above and below" (*HESP*, II, 234). Though he "looked upon" Parliament as Napoleon back from Egypt did upon the Directory, Cromwell had scruples unknown to the Corsican, who was indifferent to past or future, for "the present was his prize and spoil" (*HESP*, II, 234).

More extensive and fascinating is the correlation of Napoleon and Marlborough. Even small details are discussed; Churchill was pleased over the coincidence of Marlborough, like Napoleon, aiming at Brussels, seeking "a decisive victory beforehand" (*HESP*, III, 46), and finding himself at Waterloo. But the main item is that Churchill adjudges Marlborough's achievements comparable only with those of the other great generals of modern history, Frederick and Napoleon. Marlborough's aiming at the battle rather than the fortress as the decisive theater, as well as his aggressiveness, were anticipations of the ways of Frederick and Napoleon. Rossbach and Austerlitz were reminiscent of Blenheim and Ramillies. The two generals "were remarkable for the economy with which they managed their armies" (*M*, I, 415), but Marlborough made money go further than either did. Like the others, he lived in the field with simplicity. His ways with his troops, no less than his "simple, ruthless" strategy, may well have set the pattern for the Frenchman, for Napoleon's appreciation of Marlborough as soldier was so profound that a history of the latter's campaigns was written under the Corsican's direction and supervision.

In some ways, Marlborough was superior. He knew what Napoleon did not, that a "land commander cannot drive a fleet." Like the Corsican (and Frederick), Marlborough could interest himself in small as well as great things during a crisis, but unlike Napoleon (and Cromwell) he was not detached from battlefield suffering. He differed also in his phlegmatic, taciturn demeanor, his matter-of-fact style eschewing the "splendid invocations" of the Corsican, while his giving troops to Prince Eugene and relegating himself to an ancillary role is the reverse of Napoleon's way. Marlborough toiled for Britain, queen, and Protestantism, not for the selfish prize of empire.

Napoleon also functions as an example of the autonomy which Marlborough lacked. Though "no commander wielded such widespread power in Europe" (*M*, I, 15) until the advent of Napoleon, Marlborough had the heavier burden for lack of the authority of the other generals. Only he, among the great captains of history, was denied at headquarters or at home an unfettered command and freedom of action. If the Englishman had had the power of a Napoleon (or Frederick), the war would have been decisively finished in 1705 with a stable European peace. Time and again, in assessing Marlborough's basic procedure, Churchill says something like, "This simple, ruthless theme, applied with the highest technical skill, and with cool judgment in the measuring and timing of events, exactly harmonizes with Napoleon's processes" (*M*, I, 799).

A curious thing happened during the composition of the *Marlborough.* A new would-be entrant to the exclusive club of warriors-statesmen-diplomats appeared in the form of Adolph Hitler. If in the 1930s, Churchill's historical studies resulted in a preoccupation with his own ancestor (and, to a lesser extent, with Cromwell) and in recurring comparisons with Napoleon, in the *Second World War* it became a contemporary's turn to be compared to the Corsican, notwithstanding Churchill's earlier conclusion that the day of great generals was gone. Hitler was, of course, no field general, but the magnitude of his leadership and conquests invited such discussion. This "ferocious genius" with a "theatrical sense of history," a "power of fascinating men," a "judgment and daring" (*SWW*, I, 261), and a willingness to run great risks, by outbluffing everyone and achieving unprecedented power over a nation, was comparable—even though lacking military ability—to Napoleon.

Churchill sees Hitler assuming direct control of state policy and of the military machine, like Napoleon after Austerlitz and Jena, but by means of diplomatic and political triumphs based on daring and judgment rather than by means of military success. Hitler then confronted the British across the channel, like, 135 years earlier, Napoleon, with his Grand Army and flat-bottomed boats waiting at Boulogne for a year ready to invade. Thus, of the British fights against Philip II, Louis XIV, Napoleon, and Wilhelm, the one with Napoleon most resembled the current one against Hitler. By an "unscrupulous policy of aggression" and "swift, crushing military strokes," the Corsican had mastered Europe and its resources. But he knew, according to Churchill, that his achievement was incomplete as long as Britain remained unconquered. This familiar story obtained a new interest as a result of the events of 1940, and an awareness of the overcoming of the earlier peril was fortifying during the Battle of Britain.[8] When Britain was once again "at one time left alone to face the world" (*M*, II, 995), the recollection of Pitt's voice was most reassuring and stirring.

But, like Napoleon in 1804, Hitler lacked "command of the sea" (*HESP*, III, 244) and "recoiled from the assault of the island until at least the Eastern danger was no more" (*SWW*, II, 577). (For a while early in the war, Churchill thought—or wished to believe—that Hitler's invasion of Scandinavia was an error comparable to Napoleon's of Spain.) Though outraged by Franco's evasiveness, Hitler was not prepared to duplicate Napoleon's error of getting bogged down in Spain while invading Russia. Even as Napoleon had studied Charles XII's campaign, so "in the twentieth century another more ruthless dictator was to study Napoleon's errors" (*HESP*, III, 275). In the event, that precedent and study made no difference. In deciding to settle with Russia before the climactic destruction of Britain, Hitler was "obeying the same forces and following the same thoughts as Napoleon" (*SWW*, II, 577). Russia's supreme advantage of geographic depth once again proved her salvation, and "like the supreme military genius who had trod this road a century before him, Hitler now discovered what the Russian winter meant" (*SWW*, III, 536). Even genius errs.

Churchill was often struck by the similarity of the Napoleonic era to his own time, with a French instead of a Russian Revolution, French instead of German conquests. In the Napoleonic Wars, as now, Britain headed, after that one year alone, an encircling alliance against a land-locked military power on the continent. The United States entered both contests, albeit on different sides, while Russia left both and then was dragged in willy-nilly by the conqueror's sudden, daring, and ultimately insensate march to Moscow. These "indescribable perils" were ultimately overcome—at any rate to Churchill if not to other historians—by English vigor above all. The analogy may seem factitious to observers but, having drawn parallels between World War I and Napoleon's (as well as Marlborough's) wars and then between World Wars I and II, Churchill could not avoid closing the circle, rounding off the syllogism.

In the *Second World War,* he reveals his enjoyment of repeated viewings of the film *Lady Hamilton* (set in the Napoleonic era), as well as the Russian film *Kutuzov.* Many minor parallels with the earlier era occurred to him, and Waterloo was signally on his mind. A decisive air battle took place, like Waterloo, on a Sunday. The tensions of the Battle of Britain recalled Wellington's wishes at Waterloo, "That God or Bluecher would come!" (*SWW,* II, 456)—only this time the British did not want Bluecher. Churchill would have artillery stand and face tanks as Wellington's men at Waterloo withstood the cavalry. The Sicilian operation, indeed the war itself, reminded Churchill of Wellington's judgment on Waterloo, "a damned close-run thing." The prompt violent British attack on the Danish fleet in neutral Copenhagen, while arousing a storm at home, was vindicated by events, for two days after the navy left Britain Napoleon gave an ultimatum to Denmark. "Had the British government not acted with speed the French would have been in possession of the Danish Navy within a few weeks" (*HESP,* III, 257). In almost exactly the same way Churchill had, in a controversial and painful decision in 1940, to act to destroy the French fleet in North Africa lest it fall into Hitler's hands.

Insofar as the Battle of Britain was the finest hour of both Churchill and Britain, it could be made to correspond, in Churchill's febrile historical imagination, with the battle fought at Waterloo by the man who was at once Churchill's personal hero and Britain's noblest and most powerful foe. It was as if in some mystical sense, by beating back Hitler, Churchill were participating in the defeat of the great man the German was incompletely imitating—as if Churchill had circuitously and at long last achieved Napoleonic grandeur by rebuffing a would-be Napoleon.

Churchill realized, to be sure, that "no historical analogies can be exact." For one thing, he did not wish to insult the dead by comparing Hitler to Napoleon. If the latter took with him the noble ideals of the French Revolution, the former stood only for repression. A Nazi victory would be much worse than Napoleon's, for, as Europe knew, "Napoleon could construct as well as destroy." There was no likeness between the "Nazi system and the Napoleonic Empire" in the scale of civilization, nor ultimately between the two leaders. Lacking the Corsican's military acumen, Hitler committed "extraordinary blunders" which—Churchill asserts inconsistently in the heat of wartime rhetoric—are the one and only common denominator between the "great Emperor" and "this squalid caucus boss and butcher" (*DoL*, 189). Perhaps for moral reasons, Churchill had no doubt that Hitler's empire would "pass away as swiftly as, and perhaps more swiftly than, did Napoleon's empire, although, of course, without any of its glitter or its glory" (*BST*, 356).

That Napoleon, however angelic and superior to Hitler in many ways, shared some traits with the German and was less than perfect vis-à-vis Marlborough may remind one that he was as superlative in negative attributes as in positive achievements; and Churchill does not shrink from revealing them. For one thing, Napoleon's disregard of life has been outdone only by modern generals. For another, he was, despite his genius, a man who made mistakes and suffered setbacks. He sometimes underestimated his enemies: he discovered after Jena that Germany is "fertile in military surprises" (*WES*, 150). And not only Germany. In 1895, as a young observer in the Cuban War, Churchill watched an army of 200,000 Spaniards moving "like Napoleon's convoys in the Peninsula, league after league, day after day, through a world of impalpable hostility, slashed here and there by fierce onslaught" (*MEL*, 83). "Nothing like" the Spanish rising against Napoleon "had been seen before" (*HESP*, III, 258). Napoleon could have quit Spain without great loss, but, a conqueror needing momentum, "he feared to retreat from a false and dangerous position. He must move, like all dictators, from one triumph to another" (*HESP*, III, 260). Then came an even worse error: in the 1930s, Churchill saw the Japanese, by invading China, "repeating Napoleon's experiment of marching to a Moscow" (*SbS*, 260). (Later, of course, he saw Hitler do the same thing literally.) The result was the "most celebrated and disastrous retreat in history" (*HESP*, III, 275). Finally, internal stresses destroyed the "great Napoleon's" empire (*SbS*, 181). Even it, "with all its faults and its glories, flashed away like snow at Easter" (*US*, 123). Ultimately—and to Churchill appropriately—the story of Napoleon, the French foe, had a tragic ending, unlike that of Marlborough, the hero of Britain and ancestor of Churchill: the "fair end" to Marlborough's life is contrasted with Napoleon's "rotting" (*M*, II, 1037) at St. Helena.

Thus the lifelong obsession with Napoleon came to fruition at the climax of Churchill's career, after a half century of activism or of, as many thought, aping and mimicry. Now he himself, if he did not succeed in becoming, as he had hoped, some sort of Napoleon, instead confronted, by one of those curious ironic twists of history, another overreacher—and by his greatness in adversity helped bring about that man's Waterloo. Worship of the Corsican, no less than the ancillary lifelong obsession with the career of Marlborough, helped Churchill see events in perspective, retain his nerve, and calmly analyze the problems, not at all unfamiliar to him at least, presented by the Hitler phenomenon.

Despite the superficial differences caused by technological change, Churchill saw that past and present remain part of a single entity and that study of the past is necessary for proficiency in the present. Though reading up on all of British history, he, like a graduate student, selected certain periods for specialization. Considering what destiny had in store for him, he chose with uncanny foresight the wars of Marlborough and of Napoleon. He vaguely dreamed throughout his life of emulating both men. Then history forced a choice on him, as a would-be Napoleon suddenly sprang up, and Churchill had to follow, as best as he could, in the footsteps of Marlborough. Since the latter was his ancestor, there was poetic justice here.

But it must be stressed that Napoleon had for Churchill a duality that Marlborough did not. In his capacity as ruthless conqueror (a trait he shared somewhat with Cromwell and not at all with Marlborough), he prefigured the evil Hitler and the mortal danger that Britain and Churchill had to overcome. In his capacity as military genius, a morally neutral quality denied Hitler and shared by Marlborough (and somewhat by Cromwell), he served as a model for Britain and Churchill in

overcoming that danger. The interest in Napoleon, which in
most other people would have been an eccentricity or hobby,
was for Churchill an extended program of study in the art of
war and in the means to achieving greatness. The morally
neutral side of Napoleon became to Churchill what Jesus is to
the Christian or Bach to the musician—a hero, a teacher, a
model, and ideal by which to measure the often large failings
of lesser men striving toward the same goal. Churchill's writings are the record of that study, preparation, and fulfillment.

CHAPTER 5

# "A Cross of Thought or Action": One Man's Philosophy

## I  Between God and Machiavelli

THE themes and refrains of the previous two chapters have
to do mainly with the external world, the realm of politics
and wars, domestic and foreign policy. The critical reader ex-
pects from any writer something also touching the inner self,
the reactions of that self to its experience—that is, "philosophy" and "psychology" in the broad sense. Churchill is not
very searching in such matters, and what may be a strength in
the pragmatic politician is a weakness in the writer taking
stock of men and events. His metaphysical statements—his
commitment on questions like God, destiny, good and evil,
human nature—are sketchy or inconsistent, as when he asserts
that man is unteachable and yet expresses confidence that the
world would choose recovery rather than self-destruction. Was
he, for instance, a Christian? In 1943, he expressed himself in
Cromwellian language which left the House of Commons un-
clear whether he parodied or earnestly expressed religious
conviction.[1]

Certainly in the *Second World War,* he senses a great force at
work. There are simply too many lucky strokes and coinci-
dences, and these generate in Churchill "a feeling of interference," of "some guiding hand" which favors Britain and the
Allies for serving "a great cause" (*EoB,* 257) and for combat-
ting the "Satanic forces that have set at nought all the laws of
God and man" (*OtV,* 74). He likewise found in America's entry
into the war "much to fortify the faith of all who believe in the
moral governance of the universe" (*SWW,* III, 670). His
egoism meshes nicely with his moral reading of events: "Once

again I had the feeling of being used, however unworthy, in some appointed plan" (*SWW*, III, 671).

This higher force visits retribution on the evildoers, and those who oppose the Allies are punished, for "the wages of sin is death" (*OtV*, 229). Churchill can wallow in such pieties: of Mussolini and Ciano, he said, "See how those who stray from the true path are deceived and punished" (*OtV*, 231). He moralizes much on the "vanity of human calculation." Early in his career, he had noted, in describing counterproductive French intrigues, "a Nemesis that waits on international malpractices, however clever" (*RW*, I, 177). This moral Nemesis will reappear fifty years later, and the moralizing will grow stronger. "The wicked are not always clever, nor are the dictators always right" (*SWW*, III, 368). Their misdeeds would find them out; a day of reckoning would come. A government without scruples "seems to gain great advantages and liberties of action, but 'All comes out even at the end of the day'" (*SWW*, I, 394). Of the negotiations in 1941 among Russia, Germany, and Japan, he says, "These three coldly calculating empires made at this moment mistakes disastrous alike to their ambitions and their safety" (*SWW*, III, 195). Of Darlan's casting his lot, for reasons of personal ambition, with Vichy rather than London, he says, "How vain are human calculations of self interest!" (*SWW*, II, 230). A "guiding hand" visits retribution upon the evil doers, often—as he remarked also of the Germans in the *World Crisis*—by means of the very weapons and cunning by which they have thrived. The German defeat is in part attributed to their "crimes" (the attack on Belgium and the unrestricted U-boat war). As a historian of Britain, Churchill often censures individual and group with moral terms like "sordid and vicious," "trimmers," "shameful," "treacherous."

Yet Churchill inconsistently dismisses other people's moral delicacy and cannot stomach a politics adulterated with such sentiment. Gladstone especially (like Cromwell and those Puritans) irritates him by wearing his conscience on his sleeve and "rousing moral indignation both in himself and in the electorate" (*HESP*, IV, 219). With relish, Churchill exposes the breakdown of this frail guideline in the Gordon affair: The general, sent to oversee the evacuation of the Sudan, turned out to have scruples of his own; if annexation by Egypt of the Sudan was "repugnant" to Gladstone's "Liberal conscience," Gordon thought it equally immoral to allow the Sudanese to continue their slave trade.

If such references to higher or moral powers imply a Christian outlook, the other side of Churchill is aggressive and truculent. When it came to fighting wars, he was content to set his moralizing aside. How could he reconcile this belligerence with his Christian conscience? He rarely tried to. As in all too many others, the Christian and the warrior lived separately, in hermetically sealed chambers of the mind. After all deference has been paid to the Sermon on the Mount, the statesman must, he believes, confront higher obligations. In the attempts to avoid war, "in the last resort the use of force should not be excluded," and once force becomes necessary it should be used under the most favorable conditions. Postponing a war through pacifism is misguided if "when it comes, it is a far worse war or one much harder to win" (*SWW*, I, 320). And the conflict itself has to be "more like one ruffian bashing the other on the snout with a club, a hammer, or something better" (*SWW*, I, 587). He therefore favored massive retaliation; bombing of sensitive areas like Rome, the Cassino monastery, German-occupied France; and even the use of the A-bomb. His conclusion is dour: as was the case at Munich, "honor does not correspond always to Christian ethics" (*SWW*, I, 321), and pacifism is "the miserable sentiment which degraded our country before the war and played a recognizable part in bringing these miseries upon the world" (*SWW*, IV, 895).

Such an unsentimental outlook is part of a distrust of human nature, an attitude shared by Machiavelli when developing a secular science of politics. And on political matters, Churchill indeed often sounds Machiavellian. To be sure, except in Utopia, all politics is, almost by definition, Machiavellian. The Florentine, as has often been noted, merely recorded memorably what politicians have always intuited and spontaneously done. Those few politicians who bother to write about their art usually reverse Machiavelli's modus operandi by portraying what should have been rather than what was. Churchill was not above doing that too. But he differed from other politicians in being more voluminous and sometimes more outspoken, so that the Machiavellian element in his thought is visible. Whether he actually borrowed these ideas or independently arrived at them is a moot point. He relished the *Prince,* copies of which he gave to friends in 1908-1911, and Machiavelli, as Churchill said of the Romans, "often forestalled" many of his "best ideas" and must be conceded the "patent rights" (*MEL,* 331) on various maxims.

Machiavellian surely is his assessment of greatness. The genuineness of a prophet, Churchill declares in his early *River War* with reference to the Mahdi, who stirred up the original Sudanese rebellion, can be measured only by success. Therefore Churchill dissents from popular opinion and holds rather that, if prosperity were to come to the Sudan in the future, the Mahdi will be "the foremost among the heroes of his race" (*RW,* I, 56) and, to the Westerner, not so easily distinguishable from an Old Testament prophet rescuing his people in distress. Years later, Churchill overlooked moral issues and national interests to make an objective, admiring assessment of Hitler qua political animal, patriot, man of action: "One may dislike Hitler's system and yet admire his patriotic achievement. If our country were defeated, I hope we should find a champion as indomitable to restore our courage and lead us back to our place among the nations" (*SbS,* 144). This is the detachment and amoral perspective of the social scientist.

On specific issues, Churchill adopted the Machiavellian approach. The Florentine believed that the morale of the population rather than armaments and fortresses constituted the best defense of the state. So did young Churchill, when attacking a policy that emphasized armaments and foreign adventurism in lieu of domestic reform, decry the supposition that security rested on military preparations and "the mere multiplication of ironclad ships" (*LSP,* 295). In the 1930s, he believed that the disadvantage of having British cities and towns bombed by the new air weapon would be more than balanced by the moral advantage that the destruction would bestir everyone to fight on against such an enemy. "There is no high explosive so powerful as the soul of a free people" (*SbS,* 231).

Machiavelli and Churchill agreed also in seeing nations interact according to laws as inexorable as the laws of physics. Machiavellian is Churchill's prediction that an Italy relying on Germany for her defense would, in case of victory, be "the minor attendant, a dependency of the Nazi power" (*SbS,* 308).

Machiavellian as well is Churchill's approval of Edward IV's foreign policy of alliance with the "second strongest state in Western Europe," for to be the ally of France was to be in its power, whereas to join Burgundy "was to have the means of correcting French action" (*HESP*, I, 338). Machiavelli often asserts also that when a war is unavoidable, deferment and temporizing merely allow the rising hostile power to grow strong. "Irresolute princes, to avoid present dangers, usually follow the way of neutrality and are mostly ruined by it." So had Churchill argued in 1914 and the 1930s that a yielding to the German ultimata would merely postpone, not avoid, war.

Churchill's skepticism about the proficiency of the military professionals may be based as much on a reading of Machiavelli as on personal experiences. In asserting the superiority of tanks over cavalry (or in watching generals resist the helmet, the Stokes gun, and other innovations), Churchill found himself in the predicament described by Machiavelli: though the infantry was superior to cavalry, the rulers of the day abided by the clichés and truisms of the current experts. Similarly, the Churchillian leitmotiv of placing wartime powers in as few hands as possible rather than diluting them through the committee system may be partly Machiavellian in origin; the Florentine attributed the survival of Rome to her institution of dictatorship in times of peril, for peacetime republican practices, taking time and dependent on consensus, are inadequate in emergencies requiring prompt action.

No less important in Machiavelli's outlook is flexibility and spontaneity, keeping options open, improvising, being alert to the constantly changing nature of political reality. If, in his first books, Churchill speaks of the importance of seizing a town when the chance presents itself, despite the original plans or orders, nearly fifty years later he was interested in the possibility of "ripe plums" to be had easily while everyone's attention was riveted on the main Normandy invasion battle. He criticized the Germans and the Americans for being unable to improvise once their "overall strategy" has been established. "The best generals arrive at the results of planning without being tied to plans" (*MEL*, 213). One recalls Machiavelli's famous image of Fortuna as a woman to be tamed by daring young men—a passage echoed by Churchill: "She [the world] was made to be wooed and won by youth. She has lived and thrived only by repeated subjugations" (*MEL*, 60).

Men must therefore be open to changing events and favorable developments. In his social reform phase, young Churchill urged making alterations in the structure of society precisely in those periods of tranquillity which cause most people to be satisfied with the status quo. In that way, the terrible "Either / Or; Too Little, Too Late" predicament is avoided. "How often in the history of nations has the golden opportunity been allowed to slip away! How often have rulers and governments been forced to make in foul weather the very journey which they have refused to make prosperously in fair weather!" (*LSP*, 55). So also in the English Civil War does he see General Monk, a man "not in a hurry," saving England by knowing how to use time, flowing with the current, and acting at just the right moment. Flexibility of method in dealing with new situations is "the essential counterpart of a consistent and unswerving purpose" (*EoB*, 45).

Implicitly Machiavellian is Churchill's approving description of Henry II's domestic policy—cloaking "innovation in the respected garb of Conservatism," respecting existing forms, opposing custom to custom, stretching "old principles to take on new meanings" (*HESP*, I, 158). Flexibility in use of resources and choice of weapon is equally important. Hence Churchill approves of Alfred's use in foreign policy of money *as well as* arms and disapproves of Ethelred's *substitution* of money *for* arms. The latter grew dependent on "it in ever-increasing quantities, with ever-diminishing returns" (*HESP*, I, 101), obtaining "only the result of appeasement from weakness" (*StT*, 156). Marlborough was amply endowed with flexibility; the British government exhibited it in settling the Boer War (achieving "brilliant" results by a "singular inversion") and on Ireland in the 1910s; Churchill himself shifted, in a career of sixty years, a half dozen times in his attitude toward Russia. The cause was not inconsistency but a pragmatic adjustment to changing circumstances. Where the idealist goes down with the ship of consistency, the Machiavellian makes pacts with the Devil for the sake of survival.

Once battles and wars are won, there is a special, if rarely appreciated, way of handling the results. In one of his rare references to the Florentine, Churchill says that, after Edward

I smashed Scottish resistance, he "anticipated the teachings of Machiavelli; for to the frightfulness of Berwick succeeded a most gracious, forgiving spirit which welcomed and made easy submission in every form" (*HESP*, I, 223). Churchill was glad that after the bitter Boer War Britain resorted to a generous peace settlement in lieu of a "harsh policy of unconditional surrender" (*LSP*, 69). Likewise a strong Allied stand in 1932-1933, followed by magnanimous gestures, could have resolved tensions, for the time to make concessions was when Germany was weak, not when such acts would be misinterpreted. Caesar's conquests "were due almost as much to his clemency as to his prowess" (*SWW*, VI, 631). Churchill therefore opposed the "hang the Kaiser" campaign and the Nuremberg and de-Nazification trials.

As is always the case with Machiavelli, a choice is judged not on moral but on pragmatic grounds. Magnanimity is often expedient. Respecting local religions enables Britain to divide and rule in India. Respecting the traditional Taal dialect of the defeated Boers enables Britain to achieve peace, according to Churchill, whereas to proscribe it would be to turn its use into a protest against an intolerant act and so give it new life. He felt vindicated by the loyalty to Britain generated among the Boers by the indulgent treatment accorded them. What distinguished the successful British Empire from all others was its enlightened administration; men like Chatham knew that concessions and freedom were the only practical colonial policies. In war, as well, "giving quarter did not arise from feelings of humanity" but from practical considerations: "desperate men cost too much to kill." Similarly, the Emperor Julian was the toughest opponent of Christianity because he did not persecute. The *History* takes special note of the few wise men who have understood this principle; in America, for example, the assassinated Lincoln alone could have "added to the triumphs of armies those lasting victories which are gained over the hearts of men" (*HESP*, IV, 203). Churchill is therefore chagrined that Franco has not realized how advantageous it would be for him to offer "fair terms of surrender to beaten foes" (*SbS*, 41); instead of the wise Roman way, "spare the conquered and war down the proud," the modern practice has been to "punish the defeated and grovel to the strong" (*ItB*, 453).

## II  *Moral Hardness*

Central to the vision of Machiavelli was the choice of the imperfect but viable approach in lieu of the perfect but unviable. As he put it definitively: a safe policy does not exist, and avoiding one difficulty brings the ruler into others. "Prudence consists in being able to know the nature of the difficulties, and taking the least harmful as good." Survival may require grim actions which idealists and sentimentalists cannot bring themselves to face. Machiavelli approves of the Roman decision, after the disaster of Cannae, to refuse all aid to allies. Exactly like Churchill deciding in 1940 to withhold the last British squadrons from a falling France, the Romans were wise to refrain from a hopeless defense, in which "they would have sacrificed both their friends and their own strength, whilst as it was they only lost their friends."

Most people are afflicted by some sort of sentimentality or monomania, whether of a moral, political, or strategic nature. These are hurdles which the great man knows how to overcome. Churchill often celebrates such spiritual athleticism, as in the biography of his father: any fastidiousness over gaining political victories by combining divergent political interests Randolph found to be "excellent moralizing" but inapplicable to politics because conducive to weak proceedings. "Discriminations between wholesome and unwholesome victories are idle and impracticable. Obtain the victory, know how to follow it up, and leave the rest to the critics" (*RC*, I, 233). The language is Machiavellian; as the Florentine put it, first determine the actions and then the words.

The folly of idealism was evident at the Peace Conference of 1919, where the Americans sought to do away with the venerable system of secret meetings among the leaders of the few big powers in favor of an open forum of all allied states, large and small. This innovation not only did not work but, by delaying the unavoidable private summit conferences, helped make the final peace treaties defective. Similarly, after World War II, decrying sentimentality about small nations and secret clauses, Churchill urged frequent summit meetings of the big powers as a way of preventing misunderstandings. So also did he always espouse the "spheres of influence" policy, with all that it entailed. He would glady give China to Japan, Cyprus to

Greece, and the small East European states to Russia in return for Japanese and Greek entry into World War I and Russia's destruction of Bolshevism.

Noting that the Puritans leaned more on the Old than the New Testament, Churchill remarked that the puritanical old Rockefeller, had he followed the New Testament, would have been bankrupt. Making money is nothing in itself but, if it is pursued for the sake of power and good works, may justify even unscrupulous methods. In objecting to Prohibition in America, Churchill excoriated the repulsive idealists who ignored all the corruption that ensued from their works and yet were squeamish about tax money coming from wicked alcohol. The only effect of such measures is to bring the law into disrepute among the many who see no harm in violating it. Follies tending to vice are easily checked; follies sustained by ideals set up "sinister reactions" and create hypocrisy and a lower, not higher standard.[2] Even the writing of history is affected. Churchill dismissed Victorian historians flourishing when England was all-powerful for criticizing the deviousness of her seventeenth-century foreign policy. They forgot that a weak and threatened state has no alternative and that probity is a luxury which only states with wealth and security can afford.

Above all in combat did Churchill argue that moral discriminations could not be allowed to hamper Britain and her Allies. Throughout World War II, Churchill, with eye on victory rather than purity, infuriated idealists by making questionable alliances—with Communists, monarchists, Vichyites, dubious Italians and Germans. "In a war like this, power has to be used irrespective of anyone's feelings. If we win, nobody will care. If we lose, there will be nobody to care" (SSS, 35).

The supreme sentimentality may be the inability to confront the need to shed blood. Machiavelli defines as feeble a prince unable to carry on war; humility is not only useless but may actually be suicidal in the face of insolent or contemptuous men. Such reasoning lay behind Churchill's insistence that British reluctance to arm in the early 1910s and the 1930s was or would have been misread by Germans as effeteness and weakness. Similarly, the gentlemanly and peaceful Irish leaders who preceded the determined Parnell were futile: "Never were courtesy and reason more poorly served," for they "received that form of respect which, being devoid of the element of fear, is closely akin to contempt" (*RC*, I, 84-86).

If Machiavelli said that a prince who is cruel may in the long run be "more merciful than those who, from excess of tenderness, allow disorders to arise," Churchill reasoned that to stand up to the dictator might be hazardous but that evasiveness only meant having to do so later under "far more adverse conditions" (*WES*, 401). Sherman's Georgia campaign, he noted in 1915, should have taught Americans that sometimes a hard, scorched-earth policy is the quickest and most humane way of terminating hostilities. By contrast, Wilsonian idealism at the beginning and in the aftermath of World War I, he insists, merely prolonged the war and led to numerous difficulties. Or, in the Graeco-Turkish crisis after World War I, Britain should have compelled the parties to come to terms: "There are cases in which strong measures are the only form of prudence and mercy. . . . Knock their heads together until they settle. Such was my counsel. . . . Necessary minor but rough measures had to be taken" (*WC*, I, 436, 449). Churchill firmly approves of his father's action in dispatching a military force to re-enforce an ultimatum sent to Burma; the show of strength not only worked but allowed "no time for serious complications to develop with France or China" (*RC*, I, 524). Machiavellian surely is Churchill's sense that the periods of fiercest party strife (under Elizabeth, Anne, George III) have also been periods of maximum national vigor.[3] No less Machiavellian is the contention that necessity is a fine teacher (because, as Churchill frequently asserted, mankind is unteachable—that is, by normal means): once Britain indicated its plans to leave Palestine, "you will get attention paid to what you say and what you ask and all kinds of good solutions will immediately come into the field of possibility" (*SoP*, 195).

Growing out of the emphasis on the hard choice, the necessary bloodshed, the pragmatic philosophy is the radical either / or approach which is profoundly a part of each thinker's outlook. Since all options have drawbacks, salvation—that is, survival—is for Machiavelli not to be found in some golden mean but in a daring lunge toward an extreme. An equilibrium or precise "middle course," while in theory undoubtedly the "best to pursue," is usually hard or "impossible" to maintain. "Half-way measures are always pernicious, and never make a friend nor rid you of an enemy." In such a spirit, Churchill assesses Gladstone's fiasco in the General Gordon affair: having to choose, after military victory, between withdrawing from Egypt or annexing it as other European powers would have done, he "chose the worst of both worlds" (*HESP*, IV, 262). William III likewise "drawn by contrary calls, made the time-honored mistake of meeting both inadequately"; instead of turning all his attention to Ireland in 1689 and to the Continent in 1690, he came out of the two years with a stalemate in the latter theater and a disaster in the former. Nothing is more dangerous than "a strong policy weakly carried out" (*MFF*, 311)–or as he put it aptly in a 1928 letter: "To go half way is to pay the price and miss the prize." The post-World War II Laborite government incurred the danger, as Churchill saw it, of trying to "have things both ways," which results in "falling between two stools. Safety is not to be found in searching for the line of least resistance" or in "getting the worst of both worlds" (*StT*, 21, 27).

"Men," emphasizes Machiavelli, "must either be caressed or else annihilated." Prominent citizens of a republic should be "put out of the way" or given a share in public honors. The terrible basic choice in politics is between a ruthless but efficacious course of rule or a Christian, humane life as a private citizen; "but men generally decide upon a middle course, which is most hazardous; for they know neither how to be entirely good or entirely bad." Most leaders remain undecided and are thus crushed, whereas the Romans in all important matters "avoided half-way measures and always went to extremes."

The confronting of the necessity of shedding blood or incurring losses combines with the imperative of the either / or situation most commonly in a military context. Machiavelli declares that one should never risk his whole fortune with only a portion of his forces. So Churchill iterates that a nation or army with two separate fronts should "mask" the assailants on both fronts while organizing a "mobile central force" which is thrown in overwhelming force against first one and then the other front. Such a strategy may mean that while the main force destroys one of the enemy's armies, a defeat may be suffered by the light forces "masking" the alternative front; but "one facet of the art of war is the disregarding of secondary forfeits, however painful or disastrous in themselves" (*M*, I, 825).

The either / or dilemma has to do ultimately with timing. Reluctance to *opt for* extreme measures when success is possible results in having the same or worse measures *forced on* one when success is no longer possible. According to Machiavelli, feeble, irresolute men and governments are continually falling into this trap, and good results, if any, are accidental rather than earned. Churchill repeatedly sees such anomalies. A rebel Sudanese leader belatedly authorized an advance in the face of the oncoming British forces: "What he had not dared with 60,000 men, he now attempted with 20,000" (*RW*, I, 377). Churchill's analysis of one World War I incident—"the old Ministers had made an accommodation with their political opponents not on the merits but under duress" (*WC*, II, 401)—is carried further in his complaint that the British government in the 1930s "refused to give that guarantee when it would have saved the situation, yet in the end they gave it when it was too late, and now, for the future, they renew it when have not the slightest power to make it good" (*BST*, 58). Britain had a choice between war and shame. She chose shame, thereby making war inevitable later—and war on worse terms than would have been the case had she chosen properly.[4] The paradox is that by choosing war one avoids both it and shame but by choosing shame one obtains both it and war. Paradoxes of this sort are at the very heart of Machiavelli's philosophy (and, in different contexts, of Christianity).

Above all is his massive, loving portrait of his hero and ancestor, Marlborough, with his putative "harmony of interests" as he toiled for self, family, Britain, Protestantism, and the Grand Alliance, suffused with Machiavellian values and overtones. Marlborough earns high praise from Churchill for resorting to cunning in dealing with many agents, forces, and factions. Manipulating men through their vanities and vices as well as their virtues, he was able to bring the Dutch to fight against their will; to dangle the siege of Ingolstadt before the Margrave in order to be rid of him; to let Goslinga think that the siege of Ghent and Bruges was being undertaken on the Dutchman's own suggestion. In the debate on Peterborough's conduct, Churchill finds Marlborough's "most memorable

Parliamentary performance": an attack at once "spontaneous, dissimulating, and entirely successful" (*M*, II, 303). The speed and ease of his maneuver in the unfamiliar atmosphere of parliamentary debate "opens to us some of the secret depths of his *artful yet benevolent* mind" (italics added). In retreating from the abortive Moselle campaign in 1705, he prepared his explanation by using the very arguments on the Dutch that he had tried to eradicate from their minds. "He thrusts forward on this bleak adventure armed with the certainty of a recall, which he can use the moment that he needs it, to make his case to Parliament and to Europe. He extricated himself from all entanglements with extreme adroitness, and had an answer on every point to his critics" (*M*, I, 942). Goslinga was not wrong to speak of his "dissimulation."

Machiavelli is certainly one thinker whose name is often taken in vain. The most trivial action in personal relations is readily described as "Machiavellian," often by people who have not even read the master or whose exposure to him has been much more to the relatively limited *Prince* than to the complex, subtle, variegated *Discourses*. The descriptive, disinterested analysis in the *Prince*, with its sometimes crude and sometimes subtle psychological insights, is furthermore turned, in common discourse, into a prescriptive document replete with Hitlerian *schrecklichkeit* for its own sake. We all know what happened to Old Nick among the Elizabethan dramatists.

The consensus of scholars and political scientists is, however, that Machiavelli did not write a rationale for pathological liars (such as certain recent American presidents), for world conquerors (such as Napoleon), for egomaniacal or sadistic despots (such as Hitler), for men devious on behalf of abstract ideals (such as Cromwell or Lenin). He wrote rather as one concerned with social stability; as a pragmatist whose devotion was to the art of the possible and whose supreme value was the regeneration of the state and its survival in a healthy condition; and as a closet republican who implied (in the *Discourses*) that democratic procedures and institutions are untidy but better than all other forms of government for ensuring such survival and stability. To that extent was Churchill a Machiavellian ("artful yet benevolent" is the key phrase), far more so than most other contenders for the title and far more deeply than his famous aphorism about democracy would suggest.[5]

CHAPTER 6

# "The Accident of the Tower of Babel":
# Disunited Nations

THESE, then, were Churchill's recurring ideas on his central interests—history, politics, and war.[1] But politics, even domestic politics, and war brought Britain into relations with other nations, and his thoughts more and more encompassed the character and destinies of the world's powers. Insofar as different peoples embodied different character traits or were carried by political currents of one sort or another, these observations helped him define his sense of his own country's identity as well as his general philosophy. His pronouncements on this subject are so frequent and important as to therefore constitute another set of basic themes and topoi.

## I A Tale of Three Continents

Churchill was in fact very conscious of race and of the nation state. Despite rousing wartime oratory and identification with noble concepts like freedom, he was no cosmopolite declaiming about the brotherhood of man. History was, for him, white man's history, and, like any good Victorian, he saw the races in a hierarchy, with, at the top, Anglo-Saxon Protestant stock (coincidentally his own) administering the blessings of liberty to a turbulent Europe and of civilization to a benighted Asia, and with irremediably inferior brown-skinned Asians near, and dark-skinned Africans at, the bottom of the scale. Though he could see an ironic parallel between the Romans' regarding the Gauls as savages and the Europeans' current attitude to the Africans, he persisted in that attitude himself. The frontier war books and the *African Journey* are filled with condescending remarks about the charming if backward, docile, childlike, and irrational or inscrutable Asians and Africans. For all of his glowing rhetoric about *"Imperium et Libertas"* being "still our guide" (*Vi*, 97), he counted only the "British race" (Anglo-Saxons, whites) as citizens of the Empire. During World War I he urged the use of the vast reserves of Indians and Africans to "lighten the white man's burden" (the only time he used this Victorian phrase, albeit with altered meaning) at home; but they were not good enough to be used on the fighting line. If young Churchill defended euthanasia of the war wounded as merciful, for "extreme, prolonged and useless pain is a greater evil than death" (*RW*, II, 196), he proposed such "mercy" only for hopelessly wounded Dervish, not white, soldiers. Later he thought a nation like Ethiopia not a "fit, worthy and equal member of a league of civilized nations" (*WES*, 233). Afro-Americans fared no better at his hand; emancipation of the backward Negro in America had, he declared, as its final and inevitable result the "reassertion of local white supremacy." As a young man, he likewise thought the Cubans to be a "mongrel race" and would have America annex the isle rather than permit the rebels to form only another Latin American republic or to join Mexico.[2]

He wanted the making of silent films to be continued even after the arrival of talkies because, appealing to the whole human race and reaching primitive men, who think by pictures instead of words, they could be the means of the white man's retaining prestige and supremacy in Asia and Africa. In the 1930s, British gestures toward granting colonies autonomy seemed to him embarrassing forms of a self-abnegation that France, Holland, Italy, or America would never be guilty of, and in old age he looked with skepticism at the dismantling of the European empires. While not denying the Asians the right to self-determination, he wondered whether so much haste, bloodshed, and instability was necessary to cast off the effective administration and orderliness given by the Dutch, French, and British. Especially painful was the letting go of India. She always held a special place in his view of the Empire, as in that of his father and of Disraeli. He long argued that Britain had a moral right in India and that Home Rule would end the Empire and foolishly "force this western democratic business" (at the very time it was being rejected by many European nations) on a subcontinent with many peoples, languages, and poor, illiterate, toiling masses. It would transfer power to the local plutocrats, Balkanize the area, and, like Irish Home Rule, cause unemployment, misery, "bloodshed, tyranny, and anarchy" (*HESP*, III, 191).

If one of the traits that made India inferior was the absence, as he thought, of the martial spirit among the Hindus, Churchill, who used words like the "fatal lassitude of the Orient" (*SWW*, IV, 935), believed he discerned a like deficiency in the other giant nation of Asia. In deriding the pacifist viewpoint, he pointed to the plight of China, which, although an admirable and intelligent civilization, "always rated the profession of a soldier as among the most degraded" (*SbS*, 138). This attitude resulted in her current oppression. As a young man, he would even have added to that oppression: he believed that ultimately China would have to be tamed and partitioned by Europe. The Western nations, he later insisted, have "great establishments and businesses in China which have done nothing but good to the Chinese" (*SbS*, 139). Yet he was soon forced to reconsider this view. The invading Japanese, having expected to win by a rapid Chinese surrender, instead did for China what China could not do for itself—revive and unify the people. The Chinese had only to endure in order to administer "an exemplary discomfiture of brutal aggression" (*SbS*, 215).

Churchill's concern about China's agony in the late 1930s and the 1940s varied with circumstances. While Japan was distracted in China from any adventures elsewhere, he was coldly content to let the war there go on. Later, he feared that the collapse of China would make things difficult for Britain. Once the United States entered the war, he saw China as on the periphery of Allied interests: the Chinese were again expendable. In fact, Churchill's new optimism over China quickly turned to skepticism when he found the same optimism in America in the 1940s. With Chiang sympathizing with Indian nationalists, Churchill was moved to oppose China's future status as a fourth major power in the United Nations on the ground that it would be "a faggot vote on the side of the U.S. in any attempt to liquidate the British overseas Empire" (*SWW*, IV, 562).

Pacifism was certainly not the besetting sin of China's assailant, Japan. Here was a "martial race . . . straining every nerve" on behalf of "dreams of war and conquest" similar to the Italian and German ones; a nation where "the military mind is supreme" (*SbS*, 65). Having the missionary zeal and fanaticism of the Sudanese Dervishes and the Indian frontier tribesmen in the 1890s but armed with advanced technology, Japan stood where Rome did when first looking beyond Italy. Anglo-American relinquishment of imperial possessions in Asia would allow her to step into the power vacuum as she had, with her good but stern works, in Korea and Manchuria. Churchill consequently reserved for the Japanese epithets that smacked of racism: "evil and barbarous," "guilty and greedy," "odious," "desperate," "mad aggression," "base and squalid ambuscade" (*DoL*, 172-73, 209, 232, 42). "Once the favorite hope of the English-speaking world," which had thought that "Western science and knowledge" would integrate Japan into the modern world, Japan is now the "Land of Lost Illusions" (*SbS*, 175, 260).

Churchill was ambivalent about Japan in other ways as well. On the one hand, since Russia, Britain, and America were Asian as well as European titans, Far Eastern developments like the rise of the Japan were of great importance for Europe. On the other hand, world peace was not at all imperilled by the eruption of war between China and Japan. In fact, the Japanese invasion of China decreased the possibility that Germany would make any move which might arouse Russia so long as Japan was not free to attack Russia in the rear, and it concurrently gave the peace bloc in Europe more time to prepare itself. Hence the irony that catastrophe in the, "fortunately for us, far distant regions" was a "great reassurance" of an interval of peace in Europe. (*SbS*, 139-40). This thesis is especially tenable when one thinks, like Churchill, that Asian blood is not so precious as European.

So also did he believe in 1950 that the outbreak of the Korean war, seen in the right perspective, actually helped the chances for peace in Europe. He "never advocated sending more than a token force" (*StT*, 19) there because Communism had to be contained mainly in the West. The Korean War, one of the "local events in the Far East" (*StT*, 235) must not deflect attention from Germany, or Persia and Egypt. A worldwide Communist conspiracy, if there was such a thing, would indeed be to involve the United States and the United Nations deeply in China and thus prevent the building up of European defenses.

Churchill's notoriously Europacentric view of the world was shaped, in short, by his Victorian upbringing. When modern geographers defined Europe as only the peninsula of the Asiatic land mass, he "distinctly prefers what I was taught when I was a boy" to this "arid and uninspiring conclusion" (*EU*, 77). Europe is rather the cockpit of the world, the continent of "beautiful, fertile, and temperate lands" (*SoP*, 42); its unique "treasure of thought and toleration" (*EU*, 312), of Christianity and rationalism, has been carried to every part of the world. If it arose again, its "strength and unity would ensure the peace of the world" (*SoP*, 170).

This great continent was not unfortunately without its lethal flaws. Its "tragedy" was that though it by rights should lead, it often plunged the world into disasters. It then functioned as a foil for Britain, as the corrupt and chaotic continent from which Britain was—and, he often thought, should remain—in more than one way, detached. While Churchill applauded the growth from loyalty to tribe to loyalty to nation and while he praised nationalism as a good thing when turned to constructive uses, he preferred loyalty to continent (provided continental rivalries would not replace national ones) because excessive nationalism had been the bane of modern Europe and the cause of world catastrophe.

Another problem was that Europe was increasingly discarding its democratic principles and practices. Just when the toiling masses had, thanks to the blessings of science, for the first time a chance to live the fuller life, Churchill's dream of Britain, France, and Germany working together to make this possible was being wrenched by tyranny and aggression. After World War II, he therefore revived his dream, first delineated in the early 1930s, of something—variously called a United States of Europe, a Concert of Europe, a United Europe movement, or a European Assembly—modeled on the United States or the "English-Speaking Association." Contrasting the dislocations and barriers of a supposedly scientific modern Europe with the prosperity and growth of America, he wished for a unity such as had existed in Rome or even under Napoleon. If France properly led Germany by the hand and if Britain helped both, "these three countries, helping each other, conscious of their future united greatness, forgetting ancient feuds" (*ItB*, 247), could be the center of a revived and peace-

ful Europe, with common defense, uniform currency, and
without tariffs and barriers. The nations could better regulate
themselves through a movement with a "common European
point of view" than through the United Nations (*ItB*, 29). If he
identified himself in America as a "child of both worlds," he
also insisted elsewhere on being regarded a "good European"
(*OtV*, 235, 50). Because of their commitment to vague ideals
and indulgence in sentimental internationalist rhetoric rather
than to dealing with power realities, the League of Nations
and the United Nations did not, except for short interludes,
loom large in Churchill's thinking.

## II  *A Tale of Three Countries*

Such a movement was to include the East European satel-
lite nations but to exclude Russia. If Japan was the most European of Asian nations, Russia was, to Churchill, the most Asian
of European ones. His references to her were tinged with a
curious xenophobia and racism, and, when he expressed his
fears of the resurgence of "Russian barbarism," one cannot
always be sure if he meant "Russian" (whether czarist or
Soviet) or "Communist." Only sometimes did he distinguish
the Russian people, with their difficult peasant existence,
from their regime. After World War II, carried away by anti-
Communist rhetoric, he spoke of the "real demarcation between Europe and Asia" as no mountain chain or frontier "but
a system of beliefs which we call Western Civilization" (*EU*,
77); communism, duplicating the million-year-old white ant
society, was a philosophy for Asiatics – an assertion alike unfair
to communism and to Asia. It brought "Asiatic liquefaction"
and the "conditions of Asiatic life"; the Mongols of the fif-
teenth century did not return to Europe "till now," and no
peace could exist in Europe "while Asia is on the Elbe" (*ItB*,
50, 63). Where the actions of "Hitler and his crude Nazi gang"
could easily be forecast, the Russian oligarchs in the Kremlin,
like the inscrutable Orientals, "do not reason as we do. There
is no rational process at work which we can understand" (*EU*,
235, 373). They have "Asiatic views of the value of human life
and liberty" (*EU*, 235).

Although Russia experienced in the twentieth century
numerous rises and falls in fortune, together with a major

political transformation, Churchill's frequent shifts of policy toward her were shaped not by those internal changes but by the problems Britain faced. He was anti-Russian in the 1890s, 1900s, 1920s, late 1930s, late 1940s and conciliatory in the 1890s, 1910s, 1930s, early 1940s, 1950s. He even achieved notoriety in his reaction to Russia's watershed, the Revolution. Defending Nicholas II against charges of tyranny and incompetence, he represented the Russian populace as preferring domination by German soldiers to "persecution by a priesthood" of fanatics or by the "world-wide organization of International Communism" (WC, V, 96; VI, 378), but his only citation for that sweeping generalization were the memoirs of a lady of honor at the court! Though he himself did his best, overtly and covertly, to "strangle Bolshevism in its cradle," the new regime eventually won, partly as a result of dissension among the Allies. He was then ready to make peace with the Soviets. While "no real harmony" was possible between "Bolshevism and present civilization," an end to struggle and the "promotion of national prosperity are inevitable"; peaceful influences might mitigate the tyranny and peril. "Compared to Germany, Russia is minor" (WC, V, 401).

In the 1920s, Russia, an enigma, a titan in self-imposed exile, with tremendous military resources and hatred, lived in its cocoon as far as Churchill was concerned, but in the 1930s, he ran into a moral dilemma. The menace of communism was being eclipsed. Though he had preferred fascism to communism in Italy, the rise of an expansionist Nazi regime caused him to urge alliance with a quiescent Russia. He traced the turn in that country from Communist internationalism to Russian nationalism, from Trotskyism to a "broadening" of Russian policy, a rebirth of religion, discipline, military etiquette, a willingness to be friendly with Britain. A Russia armed to the teeth was following the foreign policy of the czars. The result, whether aimed for or not, was a resumption of the alliance of World War I, and Churchill's ideological stand against communism now underwent a subtle softening as he spoke of "perhaps not needless purges" and of generations who would have "more to eat and bless in Stalin's name" because of the autocrat's harsh measures. (SWW, I, 289; IV, 499).

At first the Western powers worried over how to keep Russia, with her secretiveness, xenophobia, surliness, and ingratitude, in the war once she had repelled the German invader from her soil. But these anxieties changed as Russia became a major military power which might impress itself on European culture and independence or which might support partisan guerillas against reactionary or monarchist groups in newly liberated countries. Yet despite his own rhetoric and the seriousness of some of the subsequent Cold War crises, Churchill argued that war was not imminent, being neither Russia's aim nor the West's. The violent abuse hurled at the West was not ominous. From Hitler all had learned that "soothing words," "non-aggression pacts" and other such attempts to "lull the democracies into a false sense of security" were the real signs of danger (*EU*, 164).

The changes in Churchill s posture toward Russia were hardly more numerous than those toward Turkey, and especially, Germany. Toward the latter, however, he brought an admiration equaled only by that for America. When he entered upon his maturity, in the 1890s, Germany was the model of precision and planning, of great military and commercial prowess. Before World War I, that "great State organized for peace and for war to a degree to which we cannot pretend" (*LSP*, 345) stood with America as our "two most important rivals," "our two great brother nations";[3] between the wars, Germany, with the resources to easily achieve "an immense mercantile ascendancy," was a "great nation united" to Britain by "many ties of history and race," the "most gifted, learned, scientific and formidable nation," which "almost singlehanded" fought "almost the whole world and almost conquered" (*SbS*, 143; *WES*, 18, 49, 141); and after World War II, she was still the "largest racial block," "one of the most powerful nations in the world, . . . an ancient, capable, and terribly efficient race" (*SoP*, 165, 232).

Germany notably stood out at the beginning of Churchill's career for her pioneering effort in welfare legislation. During his "radical" phase, he looked to the example of Germany and credited Bismarck, "perhaps more than any other," for thereby building up "in his own lifetime the strength of a great nation" (*LSP*, 374). He based various of his own proposals on the successful German system and spoke of applying a "big slice of Bismarckianism" over the underside of the British industrial

system. Even in the 1930s, Germany's aid was needed "to be-
stow a better life upon the wage earning masses in every land"
(*SbS*, 185).

Yet, at the end of his life, Churchill found that Germany had
plunged the world into three major wars in modern times, that
he had spent a "large part" of his career "in conducting war
... or preparing to do so" (*UA*, 66) against Germany, and that
he had to welcome her back among the great powers in the
wake of a "fearful second Thirty Years War" against her (*UA*,
82). Her virtues and abilities were wedded to a depravity, a
resentfulness, and, no less harmful to stability, a certain ob-
tuseness. Though efficient, the Germans were slow, needed to
plan everything, and therefore easily upset; "they could not
improvise" (*SWW*, I, 577). They had a "love of exactness, even
in regard to the most uncertain things" (*AJ*, 141). They were
"long celebrated" for "psychological blunders" (*DoL*, 157).
Despite her pioneering social legislation, Germany was also a
state where "militant socialism" had driven many into
"violent Tory reaction" (*LSP*, 78). Germany's "terrible reversion" in the 1930s was a sign of "an inferiority complex which
has rendered one of the greatest branches of the human family
singularly unsure of itself."[4]

As early as 1935, Churchill predicted the blitzkrieg. Since
Germany was "fertile in military surprises" (*WES*, 150), as
Napoleon discovered after Jena and the French at the beginning of World War I, since, that is, the "conception of
psychological shock tactics has a great attraction for the German mind," it was likely that Hitler would try to overcome a
nation in a few weeks "by violent aerial mass attack" aimed at
large cities and civilian populations (*SWW*, I, 153). Yet though
a warlike people, they were unpredictable and, as in 1918 or at
Jena, capable of sudden collapse. In the North African campaign they once again proved the saying, "The Hun is always
either at your throat or at your feet" (*OtV*, 130). They in fact
combined the traits of the warrior and the slave; unable to
value freedom themselves and hating it in others, they were
ready to trample down in other lands the "liberties and comforts they have never known in their own" (*BST*, 290). They
thus became "the prime and capital foe," hated by the end of
World War II "as no race has ever been hated" (*OtV*, 151,
187, 231).

Churchill never made up his mind as to how to locate guilt in the German community. Opposing the popular cry for the kaiser's head, he blamed World War I on the German people and "their subservience to the barbaric idea of autocracy. This is the gravamen against them in history—that in spite of all their brains and courage, they worship power and let themselves be led by the nose" (*GC*, 28). This pattern repeated itself in the 1930s. Even before Hitler's rise to power, Churchill noted that Germany's military men were "in control of the essentials" and wanted to rearm, that each concession to Germany was followed by a fresh demand (*WES*, 25). Then, under the new order, which instilled into their youth "the most extreme patriotic, nationalist and militarist conceptions" (*WES*, 141), the Germans, "always so docile in the face of a tyrant," watched the bastions of freedom go down before the Nazis "without stirring a finger" (*SoP*, 198). They were a "serviceable, ruthless, contradictory, and ill-starred race in Europe," whose latent "dark and savage furies" (*SWW*, I, 70) Hitler called from the depths of defeat.

In World War II speeches and minutes, on the other hand, Churchill stressed, perhaps tactically, that the Allies were warring on tyrannies, not races. He would help the fall of the Nazi regime by opening "a gulf between" the war criminals and "the rest of the population" (*SWW*, VI, 701). He refused, like Burke, to indict a people; they were decent patriots led by a tyrant—against whom a majority had voted—and swept by events. Indeed, after either world war, he struck a pro-German stance. Germany has a rightful place in the European family; "therefore no one has a right to describe me as the enemy of Germany except in wartime" (*SbS*, 141). Besides, if a defeated Germany and the whole of Eastern Europe joined the Bolshevik camp, 300,000,000 people armed with German science and efficiency would spread anarchy throughout Europe and Asia. European prosperity could not come by dividing or "pastoralizing" her and so relegating her to a no-man's land and to a leper's status but only by ending the thousand-year strife between her and France. Instead of punitive measures which would once again create a "poisoned community in the heart of Europe," he preferred "putting poor Germany on her legs again" (*SWW*, VI, 350). A united Europe, unable to live without Germany, had to pass "the sponge across the past. . . .

Some peoples learn wisdom in defeat," and Germany, having been twice defeated, might now play a creative role
(*ItB*, 72, 175).

If his lifetime had been spent helping keep Germany at bay,
it concurrently was spent retaining an alliance with France.
Early in his career, Churchill embarked on his lifelong cham-
pionship of that neighboring country. "Since the Anglo-French
Agreement of 1904 I have always served and worked actively
with the French in the defence of good causes" (*OtV*, 224); the
fortunes of Britain and France were, through the decades, in-
terwoven. He "understood the soul of France" and often
spoke of his old friendship with her and his love of French
culture; "whether in peace or war, in a private station or as
head of the Government, I enjoyed confidential relations with
the often changing Premiers of the French Republic and with
many of its leading Ministers. . . . They would do as much for
me as for any other foreigner alive" (*SWW*, *I*, 235, 574; *IV*,
630).

In *Marlborough*, of course, Louis XIV's France threatened
European freedom rather as, in Churchill's day, did Wilhelm's
or Hitler's Germany or Lenin's or Stalin's Russia. But much
had happened since then, France having become the land
where the Rights of Man were proclaimed and the liberties of
Europe were guarded. Since all the other European states except France had discarded their nineteenth-century political
heritage, the continuing friendship between Britain and its
"nearest neighbor," "these two great peoples, the two most
genuinely Liberal in the world" and devoted to "the great
cause" during the "ordeal of two generations," was natural
(*LSP*, 68). The French feel themselves, like Britain, the "trus-
tees" of European freedom. France, with the finest army, and
Britain, with the finest navy, being equally opposed to the
Nazi and Communist ideologies, Churchill in the 1930s called
for an open Anglo-French defensive alliance, with interstaff
arrangements; and, in the closing stages of the World War II,
he insisted on French participation in big power talks on
Germany, which would "herald a period in which she will resume her rightful and historical role upon the world's stage"
(*DoL*, 225). She was the "keystone in the arch of European
understanding which we seek to build" (*StT*, 100), because
Europe needed "some understanding and relationship be-

tween its two greatest nations" (*WES*, 52), France and Germany.

The French way of life seemed admirable or deficient, depending on one's perspective. Churchill drew one contrast between France and Spain; the latter was a backward country "cramped by the Church"; the former was—thanks to the revolution which led Europe into the modern world, gave the peasants the land, crushed the aristocracy and the church —superior in "moral qualities, in military power, in urbanity, experience and intelligence" (*SbS*, 49), in "logical and inventive genius" (*FFT*, 87). Another contrast, more frequently drawn, was between France and Britain. French politics have "an intensity, an intricacy, and a violence unequaled in Great Britain," and the affairs of the French Chamber "find their modern parallel only in the underworld of Chicago" (*GC*, 266-67). The British evolutionary process was therefore preferable to French oscillation between liberating revolution and political rigidity; the gradual, unwritten British way to the abrupt, rational, constitution-strewn French way.

## III   *A Tale of One Country*

The superiority of the British political process was only part of a larger picture. For Churchill, nearly everything about Britain was exemplary. His first books resound with the theme in an imperial setting: In India, land cultivation and population rose while the death rate sank as never before, a "monument more glorious than the pyramids" (*MFF*, 123). That the future of the "mighty continent", with its 300,000,000 people, rested in the hands of a mere 100,000 Britons filled with "pure and lofty motives" raised the British "to the level of the greatest Empires" (*FFT*, 70), present or past. A justification of the Empire and an explanation of its strength was its tolerance of all religions, no matter how "false" they be. To give some idea of the British achievement, he conjures up a Europe ruled for generations by a council which, using only 50,000 troops and 1,200 officials, achieved population increases, established laws and justice, and enabled "many nations, races, and religions"—like "Russians and Poles, French and Germans, Austrians and Italians, Protestants and Catholics, Communists and Conservatives"—to coexist peacefully. "That certainly would have been regarded as a blessed era, a kind of Age of the Antonines" (*SoP*, 234-35).

Because of her administrative gifts, "high civic virtues," and the "British art of 'muddling through,' " moreover, Britain was eminently fitted for the job of bringing civilization to the natives (*AJ*, 5). The "only true aristocracy" are the bright, idealistic young men with "famous names" who, eschewing commerce or the military, animate the Empire and spread progress. With such an enlightened officer and civil service class, the Empire rests securely on beneficence and justice. In Africa, British officials, instilling in the natives an idea of "impartial justice," "regard themselves as the guardians of native interests and rights" (*AJ*, 37). In Asia, Palestine was (until 1934) "a credit to our administration," with its initiation of roads and schools, its fostering of land cultivation, prosperity and peace; "the country had gone ahead by leaps and bounds" (*SbS*, 254). And Shanghai was turned from "mud flats" into a "noble port and city" by British "enterprise and thought" (*SbS*, 139).

Certainly this sense of empire colors Churchill's interpretation of his ancestor's actions. What Marlborough established—British naval supremacy, the foundation of British dominions in the New World and Asia—seemed the "appointed inheritance of the islanders" (*M*, II, 473). In wartime, the Empire, with the joint effort of heterogenous groups, underwent a special test and glorification. In writing of the Boer War, World War I, and Marlborough's wars, Churchill rejoiced in the peculiar nature of the British Army. Every regiment in the service and every colony in the Empire being represented in a united effort, each group was a microcosm of imperial federation. The British Army in Italy in World War II, composed of Canadians, New Zealanders, South Africans, and Indians, was the most representative of the Empire ever. He exulted in the mysterious sentiments which brought every part of the Empire zealously to Britain's rescue—feelings "unseen, unnoticed, immeasurable, far below the surface of public life and political conflict," feelings of a union based on a free way of life "reinforced by tradition and sentiment," not dependent on any written treaties (*DoL*, 69-70). And after World War II, the Empire, "this astounding union of communities and races spread around the globe," seemed to him-

—as to no one else!—"more united and powerful than at any time in its long romantic history" (*Vi*, 96, 171).

The source of this greatness Churchill found in the Briton's unique character and moral fiber. With their jocularity, their treating of crises as sporting matches, their decency, tolerance, and sense of fair play, their reliance, even in rebellion, on "law and order" and gradualism rather than force and radical change, their "unheroic" but "invaluable" way of compromise, of disguising change by retaining old forms, their stiff upper lip and their indomitability, their scientific ingenuity and their ability, unlike the Germans and even the Americans, to improvise, their love of "impulse and experiment" rather than, as in France and America, "political theory" and logic, the British "are good all through," and their genius springs "from every class and every part of the land" (*Vi*, 254). Marlborough, for one, was helped in his work by hardy sailors and soldiers, an independent Commons, and an inspired, zealous populace. The energy and intelligence directed to the military in France and Germany and to commerce in America "animates in our fortunate State all parts of the Public Service" (*RW*, II, 179). This spirit was equally responsible for the industrial revolution and the victory of Waterloo, both of which placed Britain for a century at or near the summit of the "civilized world."

Sometimes the British leaders themselves did not understand the traits of their own people, such as its love of candor. "We are not children to be kept in the dark, and we can take what is coming to us as well as any other country"; even as war leader, he himself hesitated to say optimistic things because "our people do not mind being told the worst" (*BST*, 257, 380). In the world wars, "acts of the spirit" enabled Britain to save "the freedom of the world and the life of our island" (*ItB*, 25); if that spirit died so would Britain and, with her, something precious to mankind. For the freedom born in ancient Greece, practised in classic Rome, and squelched in the "brutish barbarism" of the Dark Age was, he thought, revived in England, the home of the "mother of Parliaments."

He contrasted the British system with the common European one of a permanent ruling group, buttressed by the privileged classes, subjecting the many "by force of arms" or, as in Germany in the 1900s, of a capitalist-military-imperialist

"combination" confronting a "vast Socialist party" estranged
from basic state institutions (*PR*, 20). Though as a young man
he wanted Britain to join the reform movement coursing
through Europe with respect to an impoverished minority,
"sweated industries," and the establishment of labor ex-
changes, he was proud that Britain's finances were sound
while the European states went into debt to finance their ar-
mament programs. If Britain had political stability, Germany
had many socialists, and France, Spain, Russia, and Turkey
had disturbances. Later, despite the Great Depression, Britons
enjoyed the "fullest political liberty" and had "more food to
eat than any nation in Europe" (*SbS*, 296).

Life and property have remained more secure in Britain
than anywhere else. The growth of the British leisure class is
the amazement and envy of the world; in numbers and wealth,
in infinite opportunities for pleasure, culture, and freedom,
the affluent Britons are "more fortunate than any other equally
numerous class in any age or country" (*LSP*, 291). Like
America and France, Britain has millions of property-holding
citizens, but, unlike them, she has a less rigid constitution,
which is "mainly British common sense." Constitutional
crises are settled without bloodshed, and periods of fierce
party strife have been periods of maximum national vigor. The
unities in British life are far greater than the differences: the
social services have been built up by all the parties, and in
foreign affairs and national defense, "nine-tenths of the
British people agree on nine-tenths" of what is done (*StT*,
211).

Most of the workers have a better standard of living than
their counterparts in Germany, Italy, or France. Their unions
are individualist, not socialist. Britain knew the unique art of
"assimilating" the leaders of the "left-out millions." A French
ambassador is called by Churchill as witness to the fact that in
twenty years Britain underwent a revolution more profound
than the French one. That is in part because the British worker
does not dream up new systems but seeks "fairer treatment in
this one" and in part because the British genius worships custom and at the same time makes tradition bend to the needs of
democracy (*GC*, 82). That Britain is "muddled in thought and
sensible in action" is seen in the peculiar combination of democracy and monarchy, in the sovereign's being supreme yet

under the people's control. Placed, in accordance with theory, experience, and common sense, beyond ambition and politics, the throne guarantees freedom and secures against the despotisms which have overtaken ancient civilizations in Europe. The Dominions are also linked in this unique multiple kingship, and Britain has "the oldest, most famous, honored, secure and serviceable monarchy in the world" (*Vi*, 183).

That in crises Britain is ready to opt for coalition governments symbolized for Churchill the ultimate unity of the nation. "Personal kindness and good feeling" are "never far below the sullen surface" of modern British politics, which is full of health, generosity, and honor (*RC*, I, 267). Political differences "in no way prevented harmonious and agreeable relations between the principal personages" (*WC*, I, 29). This reservoir of good sense and ultimate justice prompts Churchill to solicit a final evaluation of Randolph's, Marlborough's, and his own careers not from the political parties, which were unreceptive to these independent protagonists, but from the England which transcends all factions.

The British character expresses itself in its foreign policy no less than in its domestic politics. Both in South Africa and in Ireland, Britain did not resort to a "harsh policy of unconditional surrender" but turned instead to a peace settlement (*LSP*, 69). Being, through her empire, a major power in the continents of Europe, Asia, Africa, and, through her special relations with the United States, in the Western Hemisphere as well, she has a unique role vis-à-vis Europe. She prospers only during peace, and her interests are consequently identical with larger world interests. The strong pillars of the world community which he envisioned in 1930, as well as after World War II, would be a confederation of Europe, whose resurrection from ruin the British, as "good Europeans" should want intensely; the Commonwealth and Empire, "which must ever draw closer together" (*EU*, 65); and an Anglo-American fraternal association. "These three majestic circles are coexistent" (*EU*, 82). One could be a good European only by having a strong Britain, whose Royal Navy had long protected "human progress and freedom" and Britain in turn could be made stronger by allying herself with others in a policy of collective security (*WES*, 232).

When such arrangements were not possible and war ensued, Britain was the natural leader of the forces of freedom, thanks to the Briton's love of the duties and responsibilities of leadership. Echoing Shakespeare's Henry V, he said during the grim days of World War II that the "very problems and dangers" facing their country should make Britons "glad to be here at such a time. We ought to rejoice at the responsibilities with which destiny has honored us" (WES, 73). Britain typically enters the world stage in the second sentence of the *History* by "already obstructing the designs" and "ambitions" of a rising continental military tyrant, Julius Caesar, the first of many. Churchill gloried in what ensued, in the "marvels and prodigies in our island story" (M, II, 995): that Britain had suppressed the slave trade, protected the newly independent Western hemisphere and fought for the cause of free trade and freedom of the seas; that she had never been invaded in a thousand years; that megalomaniacal Spanish, French, and German kings, emperors, and dictators had been humbled mainly by peace-loving, commonsensical Britain; that the Grand Alliance against Hitler was made possible when resistance by a solitary Britain gave Russia and America time to arm; that in times of trouble "after a prolonged peace" Britain usually found "leaders of quality and courage" (L, 495)–men like Drake, Marlborough, Chatham, and Nelson, whom he proudly evoked during the perils of 1940. With a clear policy, the prestige of victory, her power of the purse, her arsenal of munitions, her growing military strength, and, above all, her primary weapon, the navy, Britain was the inevitable leader.

The *History* accordingly traces a recurring pattern in British history. In 1778 there began a world war, and Britain was "without a single ally" (HESP, III, 164); in 1804-1806, she found herself fighting alone against Napoleon "during one of the most critical periods of her history" (HESP, III, 244). In 1914, that predicament, had it come with the fall of France and Russia, would have found her, he insisted in 1914 and in the 1930s, ready to fight on alone by sea, still able to come and go anywhere and grow stronger until she could win. And in 1940 that, of course, is exactly what happened, and he, aptly enough, was at the helm. Churchill even believed that Hitler gave Britain indirect tribute by working on a plan to destroy her, who had the honor of being his "main and foremost enemy" (BST, 335), the last obstacle "to the loot of the whole world. . . . We are the target. We are the prize" (*EoB*, 257-59). Without her resistance, the Grand Alliance "would never have come into being" (*EoB*, 108). If during that war he rejoiced in the fact that Britain was being "tried and proved to a degree which has not previously been known to human experience" (*US*, 80), after the war he sometimes skirted self-pity: "No nation has ever run such risks in times which I have read about or lived through" and "received such little recognition for it" (*UA*, 50).

In writing about World War I, the wars led by Marlborough, and World War II, Churchill reveled in catalogs of the nationalities fighting together in British armies or armies led by Britain. "Indian troops, Fighting French, the Greeks, the representatives of Czechoslovakia, . . . Malays, Burmans, Chinese, Dutch" (*EoB*, 266, 309), as well as Nepalese, Africans, Ceylonese, Americans, Dominion troops, South Africans, Brazilians, liberated Italians, Palestinian Jews, and Poles: "There has never been anything like it" (*DoL*, 155). These catalogs were his way of establishing a world community, a consensus, a majority which Britain defended, represented, led, saved, his way of validating British moral supremacy and disinterestedness in fighting "for what was precious not only for ourselves but for mankind" (*ItB*, 303). He spoke often, as had his ancestor, Marlborough, of the "common cause"; or of the "Grand Alliance," the "cause of the United Nations" (*DoL*, 91, 96, 89). Such catalogs and phrases were, of course, an expression of his romantic notions about his motherland. This belief in the triumph of honor and dignity over self-interest in the Briton is the heart of his faith. He did not realize that many of the non-European people would, upon the cessation of worldwide hostilities, turn their arms against their benevolent British masters in a fight for the same freedom which they allegedly defended against Germany or Japan.

That such acts of apparent ingratitude were actually acquiesced in by Britain, Churchill would account for by another topos: the most difficult time for Britain was not when she confronted a ruthless foe in do-or-die combat but rather in the aftermath of the inevitable success. He traced in British history an alternation of periods of heroic striving, such as under Elizabeth and Anne, Chatham and Pitt, with those of

repose, growth, or stagnation, which were "the necessary prelude for the renewed advance of Britain to Imperial state" (*M*,
II, 1028). Some such oscillation can no doubt be found in most
societies, but what made Britain unique for Churchill was that
she had had so much resilience and change, so many periods
of great constitutional and imperial gains, while her stagnant
phases lasted years or decades, not centuries or millenia.

The difficulty was in the transition periods. Sloth and decline followed in the wake of great victories and persisted in
the face of new dangers, for in peacetime the ordinary Briton
ignored the events that would crucially affect him. In 1919
Churchill complained that not for the first time would Britain
have "won the war and lost the peace,"[5] and after World War II
she had "once again cast away" by folly much that she had
gained by "virtue and valor" (*EU*, 424). He went so far as to
assert after each world war that the first postwar years were
worse even than the war years. Not at his best in peace time,
he would complain during such interludes, especially in connection with the economic problems that then plagued Britain, "We see our race doubtful of its mission and no longer
confident about its principles, infirm of purpose" (*ATS*, 240).
Britain alone passed through different moods, from "great de-
jection" to heroism and triumph and then to exhaustion.
"What has been gained with enormous effort and sacrifice,
prodigious and superb acts of valor, slips away almost unnoticed when the struggle is over" (*SoP*, 150).

Despite this one sour note in his paeans, this one major flaw
in her character, Britain is the shrine at which Churchill worships. The role of France, the glory of European civilization,
the noble "common cause" of the world war alliances, the
greatness of America (one of Britain's most dramatic gifts to
world civilization and a topic far too large to be considered
here)[6]—all these are, for Churchill, ancillary to, and brought
together by, Britain and her civilization, her destiny and mission, her vast cultural and political legacy to mankind. If there
is any one theme tying together the many books Churchill
wrote, besides the obvious one of explaining or justifying self
or family, it is the celebration of the grandeur of Great Britain.
Just as his remarks on the major European powers reveal
him—who sees only the martial spirit, the will to fight and
conquer, behind the rivalries of the empires—blissfully ignor-

ant of the role of socioeconomic forces, so do his hymns to his motherland simplify matters a little too easily. Around a rather large kernel of truth on this subject, he doggedly wrapped layers of hyperbole, distortion, complacency, and rhetoric. Hardly anything else—not his political principles, not his familial attachments, not warmaking, not power itself—seemed in his utterances to matter so much to him so consistently as Britannia Triumphant.

CHAPTER 7

# "Not Unlike Planning a Battle": Perspectives and Techniques

IN his autobiography, Churchill tells of learning that narrative writing "was not only an affair of sentences" (*MEL*, 211) but of paragraphs and chapters; the author must weave together heterogeneous incidents and establish proportion and order in the entire work. Like most writers, Churchill does not indicate the means by which this transmutation of material into literature is achieved, and even the critic, with all his analytic tools, can only suggest some of the components of an individual's style. The rest is part of the mystery of the creative process.

## I  *The Historian's Vantage Points*

Churchill brought to his work an artist's interest in construction. One sort of structure, which he said the sense of drama seeks in the lives of prominent men, is struggle, rise, triumph, reign, and fall. That is a pattern common to three of his major works, *Randolph Churchill*, *Marlborough*, and *Second World War*: governmental mistakes and the hero ignored; the hero at the helm in a critical hour: the coming of success, which brings with it the greatest disappointments and the hero's relapse into powerlessness. Another kind of structure results from the fusion of the chronicle of great events with the story of one individual's experience. Common to biography, memoirs, and historical fiction, this pattern obtains in all his books except the *History*.

A third kind grows out of his manipulation of past and present, out of the question of what constitutes historical reality—is it in the way events were perceived by the participants or the way posterity, with its detachment, accumulation of documents, and comprehensiveness of vision, sees them? No doubt because of his own prominent role in so many of the events he wrote about, Churchill emphasized the former. Whether writing the biographies, *Randolph Churchill* and *Marlborough*, or the persistently self-justifying war memoirs, *The World Crisis* and *The Second World War* (but not the *History*), Churchill attempts, through the rich use of original documents (or, in the *Commission*, the evocation of earlier states of mind), to recapture the past more than to express the hindsight of the omniscient narrator.

He eschews the "easily turned language of the aftertime" for the orders and the counsel given while the results were "lapped in the mysteries of the unknown future." Such documents "are the only foundation upon which the judgment of history can be erected. They alone reveal the perplexities of the situation at the moment" (*WC*, II, ix-x). They make questions of right and wrong decisions dependent on the knowledge then available. If "each man has his tale," his own past words tell it best and allow the reader to judge for himself. Of the fear of German invasion, for instance, he notes in the *Second World War*, "No one can understand without reading the papers written at the time how hard was the strain, and how easy it was to make decisions which might be tragically falsified by events" (*SWW*, III, 512). Even slight nuances can make a difference; hence he says in the *Commission*, "Lest my memory should embroider the tale, I transcribe the words I wrote that same evening" (*MEL*, 338).

In the war memoirs as in *Randolph Churchill*, Churchill prints various notes, memos, and situation papers dealing with possibilities and conjectures, or even letters which were not sent, such as one to Stalin, which remains "an authentic account of my thought" (*SWW*, VI, 231). Not what happened but how Churchill thought *then* is frequently the subject at hand. He offers one letter "of no particular significance" because ostensibly one can measure the Irish crisis by it, or another as "a record of that darkest hour which we are told precedes the dawn" (*WC*, IV, 185). Such a procedure presents the facts as then known, lends authenticity to the story, creates suspense, and, above all, gives the reader a unique glimpse into the workings of wartime imperial government. We are in the cockpit of power. We see not only the battle and its results, as

usual in history books, but the preparations, the difficulties
and tensions, the maneuverings—what Churchill calls some-
where the "strategic natural selection" whereby a plan of action which afterward seems to have been inevitable was
gradually arrived at by the process of elimination, compromise, balancing of factors. Then we follow the course of the
battle itself—which sometimes seems anticlimactic!—by the
dispatches from the field.

The emphasis on the presentation of original documents
and on the avoidance of the wisdom of hindsight does not pre-
clude Churchill from turning periodically to the fuller picture,
signaled by "we know now." Subsequent events and enemy
records are appealed to, usually to show how right Churchill
had been. The pathos of the opportunity missed in the Dardanelles affair is signally dramatized in this manner. After telling the story only in the light of the knowledge then available, he lifts the veil "which separates contending forces and
divides the present from the future" (WC, II, 260). The shel-
ling of the British coast in December, 1914, is described first
"exactly as it appeared" to the Admiralty at that time, "but let
us now see in essentials what had happened" (WC, I, 513).
The passage of time naturally creates ironies. Of some incidents he remarks that "it is odd that, while at the time
everyone concerned was quite calm and cheerful, writing
about it afterwards makes one shiver" (SWW, II, 418). But the
crises had fortified the soul, and though something like the
Dakar expedition was a dangerous foray, "these were days in
which far more serious risks were the commonplaces of our
daily life" (SWW, II, 477). Sometimes the reverse is true: an
event which was troublesome turned out to have been trivial.
"Had we known" that the Balkan situation would soon be relieved by Hitler's invasion of Russia, "we should have been
greatly relieved" (SWW, II, 593). Indeed, of many problems
he would say, "When I look back on all those worries, I remember the story of the old man who said on his deathbed that
he had had a lot of trouble in his life, most of which had never
happened" (SWW, II, 472).

Churchill is, in short, aware that hindsight neither can nor
should be excluded. Two views of a campaign are possible,
two sorts of narrative. Many details are "essential to the truth
as well as the interest of the account," but the reader needs

also a general idea of the whole, lest the various operations will seem "disconnected and purposeless." The overview which hindsight provides requires an understanding of the "logical sequence of incidents" resulting in a climactic "trial of strength" rather than "wild scenes and stirring incidents" (*RW*, I, 373). This narrative device of prolepsis, or foreshadowing, may add poignance to a story: the biographer of Lord Randolph often reminds us of the "melancholy conclusion" of the tragic story: "little did they know how short was the span" of life left to the hero (*RC*, II, 301). "The last five years, as they were fated to be, of his physical strength. . . . On that exciting night [he] had only five years to live" (*RC*, II, 307, 426). In giving in the *World Crisis* a specimen of Fisher's lively epistolary style, " 'Yours till Hell freezes,' or 'Till charcoal sprouts,' " Churchill jumps to the climax of the Gallipol fiasco: "Alas, there was a day when Hell froze and charcoal sprouted . . . when 'My beloved Winston' had given place to 'First Lord: I can no longer be your colleague' " (*WC*, I, 78).

Or the prolepsis duplicates the surprise of the unprepared world, as when Churchill abruptly reveals the resignation of Randolph before detailing the behind-the-scenes events that led to the act. It may heighten the importance of the story: "Cardonel's office shut down. When it reopened four days later [after Blenheim battle] the destiny of Europe had been settled for nearly a hundred years" (*M*, I, 837). Such melodramatic glances ahead often come at the conclusion of a chapter.

Besides enabling the reader to judge intelligently a decision or a character, the foreshadowing may allow a moralistic reading of events, an ironic gibe at the expense of a "villain": In the *History*, *Marlborough*, and the *Second World War*, Churchill looks ahead from the moment of the villain's triumph—Bolingbroke's or Mussolini's—to the happy end. Charles II, though seeming at the mercy of Shaftesbury, by patience and daemonic ingenuity, "emerged the victor, and the merciless Shaftesbury, stained with innocent blood, eventually died in exile" (*HESP*, II, 281). In the *World Crisis*, it casts a sense of futility over the descriptions of the vast plans, armies, battles. The narrative of the *Roving Commission*, depicting the late Victorian world in which Churchill grew up, is filled with references to the disillusioning, turbulent Boer

War and World War I. Similarly in *Marlborough*, glances at modern distresses present the Age of Queen Anne in a favorable light.

The *Second World War* like the *World Crisis*, contains three kinds of prolepses: to immediate results; to the outcome of events at war's end; and to the postwar period in which Churchill writes. The first vary; the second are nearly all cheerful; the last are uniformly depressing. An example of the first kind involves the various plans for British offensive action: "In the end all were fulfilled in the exact order designed, but not until 1942 or 1943, and in very different and more favorable circumstances than those we could foresee in October 1941" (*SWW*, III, 541). The second kind is the glance ahead to the happy outcome of the war. Mussolini is a notable whipping boy and buffoon here. His sin seems to have been less his Fascist tyranny than his not appreciating British might, and in a series of mocking choral comments Churchill juxtaposes the Italian's boasts with the fate that overtook his plans. Or, in speaking of the depressing 1940 German penetration "or 'Bulge,'" Churchill adds, "as we called such things later on," thereby reminding us that better days would yet be seen—even despite the recurrence of such a German breakthrough in that same region in 1944. Material uncovered by the end of the war also helps us assay men and events. Thus the cowardice and folly of the Anglo-French policy of the 1930s is revealed in all its starkness and irony when juxtaposed with contemporary records of the anxieties of the German (and Italian) generals.

An example of the third kind of foreshadowing is the observation, in the preface to the first volume, that not only was the war unnecessary but "we have still not found Peace or Security, and we lie in the grip of even worse perils than those we have surmounted" (*SWW*, I, v). Likewise, in describing his position on the India question and his fear of chaos if Britain were to depart, he concludes, "We have now along this subsidiary Eastern road also reached our horrible consummation in the slaughter of hundreds of thousands of poor people" (*SWW*, I, 67).

## II  *History as Background*

The historian has at his disposal as well the past or, with reference to the "new" past which he unfolds, the older, known past, the past perfect. As a lifelong student of history, a professional historian, and a statesman associated with his country's government for a half a century, Churchill could not help seeing events against the larger background. Few political and military leaders have had such a sense of the relevance of history, or at least of military and political history; few wanted everyone to realize, as he did himself, that the present generation was, in turn, on "the stage of history" and would have their deeds read about by schoolboys "a hundred years hence" (*PR*, 15). Often referring in narrative or speech to historical incidents, he heightened the significance of the present by juxtaposing it with matter from his rich historical imagination rather like a poet utilizing Greek or Christian mythology. His speeches and articles of the 1930s, with their occasional references to such recondite persons and things as Ethelred the Unready or the *Anglo-Saxon Chronicle*, reflect his massive scholarly projects of that decade. One current event seemed uncomfortably reminiscent of an embarrassing incident in the Age of Anne, which he had recently studied: "Only the other day I was reading how in 1709 . . ." (*SbS*, 142).

The present did not occur in a vacuum but was an evolution from, or a repetition of, events in the past; in the 1930s, he worked at night on *Marlborough* and during the day urged another encircling Grand Alliance against another continental tyrant. The *History* naturally contains innumerable cross references among periods and events and characters; historical parallels and repetitions abound. Thus the Roman conquest of Britain was more difficult than Clive's of India, or Alfred's life in the woods was like Robin Hood's in Sherwood Forest. Battles are often compared: Calais in the fourteenth century with Dunkirk in the seventeenth; Richard II preparing for civil war "at the very same spot where Charles I would one day" (*HESP*, I, 277). The refusal of the General Assembly of Scotland to dissolve in November, 1638, was like that of the French Assembly in 1789 (as well as the Parliament in 1681). The migration to America from England was like that to England by Saxon and Viking.

What is to be expected in a work of history addressed to those interested in books and in the past is somewhat unusual in wartime speeches addressed to the general populace or the House: discussion of health insurance is punctuated by a glance at Tudor suppression of quackery; discussion of military horrors led to references to Voltaire, Prussia, and English policy during the Napoleonic wars; of Spain, to its role as a "famous Empire" and the help the British later gave it against Napoleon; of the Maquis, to the trail-blazing French Revolution; of Holland, to its alliance with Britain in the War of the Spanish Succession. When listing in the war memoirs the locales through which the victorious allied armies passed in 1944-1945, he conjured up the great battles that had once taken place there, in Marlborough's and Wellington's wars, in World War I, and the early, disastrous phase of World War II. He could, unlike most men, look beyond the marvels of modern technology and see the tank in the context of history, whether of Hannibal's elephants or, ingeniously, even earlier: "Greek and Trojan were equal until the Greek invented the first tank, which is described by Homer as a wooden machine in the shape of a horse."[1] And, in turn, antitank weapons could stop tank charges rather as new British weapons stopped the old chivalry at Crecy and Agincourt.

In addition to aiding analysis, the historical analogy could facilitate persuasion. After the war, France seemed to him the natural leader or initiator for a United States of Europe because Henry IV of France had first forwarded the "Grand Design" of a permanent committee of the fifteen leading European nations to arbitrate disputes and take common action "against any danger from the East, which in those days meant the Turks" (*EU*, 311) and because in 1871, during the Franco-Prussian War, Victor Hugo had first spoken of a United States of Europe.[2] Obviously the military and political reasons for singling out France were of greater importance, but the historical precedent added a poetic dimension and imposed on events a pattern and logic which his sensibility, like that of most intellectuals, traditionalists, theologians, and editorial writers, craved. History also provided important polemical tools. In the wake of Gallipoli, Churchill often utilized the past in the debates the fiasco had aroused. In the *History* he cited Prince Rupert and the American Union fleet as separately proving that land batteries "could be silenced by broadsides from ships afloat" (*HESP*, II, 233). He was similarly pleased to see that Roman defense strategy in Britain, like Drake's opposition to the government's policy of dispersion all along the coast, accorded with his own strategic thinking.

His very first books evince a readiness to look at events under the aspect of history. In *Malakand*, for instance, the Mad Mullah is akin to Peter the Hermit, or Britain faces the same difficulties which Alexander, according to Arrian, confronted in his march to India. Parallels between the Roman and British empires are intimated periodically; British (and, in his 1895 dispatches, Spanish) soldiers are held to be the peers of the Romans, and General Blood is a proconsul. (In the *India* of 1931, the parallel was in the possible decline and fall of the British Empire.)

The career of the protagonist of *Randolph Churchill* is usually compared by the narrator with those of the great politicians Pitt, Palmerston, Disraeli. The crisis of 1885-1886, for instance, recalls that of 1782-1784, the period between the fall of Lord North and the triumph of Pitt: ministries rose and fell rapidly; "a new, young figure sprang suddenly into universal attention"; one of the parties entered a disastrous coalition while the other, "taking office in a minority, secured a predominance which lasted for a generation" (*RC*, I, 376). The swiftness of Randolph's rise had been "excelled only by the younger Pitt" (*RC*, II, 177). The concurrent books of Churchill's "radical" phase portrayed the proposed social reforms as part of a steady, ongoing process of two hundred years, as merely a "big step forward towards that brighter and more equal world" (*LSP*, 345) for which posterity would in turn honor the present. Whether that march forward would be peaceful or not depended on how much the other side was willing to learn from history: there was no precedent for the House of Lords rejecting a budget (Lloyd George's "People's Budget" of 1909) and too much of a parallel between the Lords' arrogance and that of the French nobility before the Revolution.

In the *World Crisis*, Churchill noted curious repetitions of history: now, as in the Napoleonic War, Britain headed an alliance against a land-locked military power. America, moreover, entered both contests, albeit on different sides, at the time of a great change in Russia's posture. After the war, the Versailles peace treaties were seen by him in the line of the monumental settlements of Westphalia, Utrecht, Vienna; Lloyd George's difficulties with the Irish question placed him in the company of Essex, Strafford, Pitt, and Gladstone. On his favorite theme of magnanimity in victory, he pointed to the few cases of its being practised: Grant at Appommattox, Castlereagh, Bismarck in 1866, the Boer War settlement.

As World War I itself entered history, it became in his succeeding works a prominent point of reference. In *Marlborough*, for instance, the hero found his vocation in the wars of 1688-1712, which were comparable only with (beside the Punic Wars) the 1914-1918 war for extent and exhaustiveness, for British leadership of an encircling alliance against a would-be continental tyrant, for the drawing in of other nations. Even the battlegrounds were often the same. The duke of York's idea of placing the Anglo-French fleet in 1672 about the Dogger Bank prompts the parenthesis, "we now know these waters as well as he" (*M*, I, 81). When the British reduced Ostend to rubble in 1706, it was "not for the last time in its history" (*M*, II, 134). Raiding French provinces, Marlborough entered "many French towns whose names have hallowed memories for our generation" (*M*, II, 400).

In writing for the first time about a relatively remote period, Churchill availed himself of comparisons and contrasts with his own age or "translated" political and military matters into modern terms. The modern aristocracy of financiers, boxers, and film actors, for example, are expected to lead model lives, whereas the seventeenth-century nobility had a looser code; hence Marlborough's sister's becoming mistress of the duke of York was not then thought of in Victorian fashion as a "dishonor" but rather as an "honor."

World War I, with its prelude and postlude, looms also over the speeches of the 1930s and of World War II. When dealing with any of numerous problems common to both wars, he spoke of "the old grounds that so many of us knew so well" (*BST*, 294). As the only man in history to hold the same prominent post, first lord of the admiralty, at the beginning of two world wars, he could hardly miss the personal dimension of the many similarities and contrasts, the eery repetitions of history. Later, the Dardanelles expedition, with its delay followed by disaster, haunted him during the taking of Madagascar in 1942 and during the Salerno and Normandy landings. The subsequent Allied thrust brought them to towns—Arras, Douai, Lille—redolent with World War I associations, and the

December, 1944, offensive by the Germans predictably duplicated the one of March, 1918.

Other wars also came to mind. In the midst of the perils of
1940, his thoughts naturally went to the ghosts of Drake,
Marlborough, Chatham, Nelson, and "those brave old days of
the past" (*BST*, 368). Battles in Persia, Greece, and Italy were
taking place amid the monuments and memories of ancient
empires and wars, as sometimes he alone knew or cared.
Marlborough being on his mind, he compared and contrasted
Montgomery with the duke.

If history provided a perspective on events and therefore a
means of endurance and of confidence, it could also be worri-
some. The American Civil War taught that men (Southerners
then, Germans now) may fight nobly even on behalf of evil
causes and even long after the final adverse result becomes
clear. Worse, Churchill recalled Athens losing to Sparta,
Carthage to Rome: "Not seldom in the annals of the past had
brave, proud, easygoing states been wiped out" (*SWW*,
II, 257).

## III  *If*

A counterpart to the foreshadowing of what would occur and
to the citation of what did occur in the distant past is the "if,"
the conjecture as to what *might* have occurred. Historians
(like, for instance, Von Ranke and Macaulay) no less than
philosophers love to indulge in this detour along one of the
roads not taken by events, this intellectual game of selecting
the "sharp agate points on which the ponderous balance of
destiny turns." As a means of shedding light on events, decisions, and actions, on the opportunities and disasters narrowly
averted, as a reminder that events in the past were once in the
future, an attempt to gauge the chances of an event on the eve
of its realization, as a recreation of the world, a toying or test-
ing of reality by means of temporarily adopted assumptions, as
a clarification of what is potential by means of reducing things
to an extreme, the "if" is "a corrective to undue complacency. . . . Although vain, the process of trying to imagine what
would have happened if some important event or decision had
been different is often tempting and sometimes instructive"

(*SWW*, II, 221). The conditional or subjunctive is a moral vacation from the indicative mood, suggesting that any point in
history is formed by a series of crossroads. Such experimenta-
tion or play of the mind is in fact crucial to the analysis of
history, for "in all great controversies much depends on where
the tale begins" (*GC*, 122).

Churchill was fascinated by the subject from the beginning.
"Every incident is surrounded with a host of possibilities, any
one of which, had it become real, would have changed the
whole course of events. . . . We live in a world of 'ifs'" (*RW*, I,
235). In one of the Boer War books he quotes from someone's
diary a speculation: "Such is the fashion of war. If so-and-so
had happened—always 'if'!" (*IH*, 346). But since conjecture is
ultimately futile, wisdom and convenience dictate the assumption "that the favorable and adverse chances equate" and
can be set aside and that, at least in the River War, "fortune
played a comparatively unimportant part" (*RW*, I, 236). In the
*World Crisis* the hypothetical conjecture is much used, as in
the description of the sweeping results if Germany had con-
centrated wholly on either Russia or France at the outset or if
the Allies had returned to the Dardanelles in 1916. The consideration of the vast changes that would have been wrought
by either a British or German victory in the inconclusive Jutland sea encounter shows it to have been a critical juncture
after all. Another is the beginning of 1917, with its "three
stupendous events"—the U-boat war, the Russian Revolution,
the American entry. "The order in which they were placed
was decisive," and juggling the sequence creates food for
thought and awe at the mysterious ways of fate: if the Russian
Revolution had come first, the other two events might not
have followed and France would have fallen. "In this sequence we discern the footprints of Destiny" (*WC*, III, 216; V,
477), and the sense of fatality is heightened by the narrator's
"if."

Conjecture is often poignant. Awesome are the "long chain
of fatal missed chances," the "terrible Ifs" at the Dardanelles.
A dozen situations beyond the control of the enemy could
have ensured success if developed differently. In the *Second
World War*, Churchill discusses how easily this most prevent-
able of wars, as he calls it, would not have taken place if
Roehm had killed Hitler or if any of a series of simple, firm

actions had been taken by the Western powers in the 1930s. Sometimes "if" serves as a source of pride: if the supplying of the Middle East Command had not begun in the dark days of 1940 amid the invasion threat at home, the Army of the Nile would have fallen during 1941. At other times it militates against excessive pride: if the London blitz had been carried out with the bombs of 1943, or if the attack had been two or three times as severe or as long, London, and with it Britain, might well have crumbled. If Germany had tried to invade Britain right after the fall of France and if Japan had entered the war at the same time; or if Stalin and Hitler had arrived at a permanent agreement, perhaps with Japan as an "eager partner," "we cannot attempt to describe what might have happened" (*SWW*, II, 587).

"If" can be a way of indicating the folly of what was done. In one of the most striking conjectures of the *World Crisis*, Churchill initiates discussion of the Peace Conference with a fantasy. "The reader may perhaps at this point be willing to study some speculative questions in a purely imaginary form. Let us then for a few moments leave the region of 'what happened' for those of 'what might have happened.' Let us dream one of the many Armistice dreams," one which contains all the things, like a summit meeting at the outset, that Churchill thinks should have happened (*WC*, V, 6). In the fashion of medieval prophetic dream visions, the fantasy ends with a shift from the subjunctive to the indicative mood: "It was at this moment that the spell broke. The illusion of power vanished. I awoke from my Armistice dream, and we all found ourselves in the rough, dark, sour and chilly waters in which we are swimming still" (*WC*, V, 12).

The dream about the Peace Conference was duplicated a few years later with a similar mental exercise about the American Civil War. "If Lee Had Not Won the Battle of Gettysburg" is Churchill's contribution to the fashionable "quaint conceit" of supposing "what would have happened if some important event had settled itself differently." This time, instead of using the common device of looking at a hypothetical reconstruction of history from the vantage point of an uncomfortable present actuality, Churchill with a deft twist turned this (as the mischievous title indicates) into a double fantasy by writing about a hypothetical nightmarish century of war and dislocations—the world we know so well—from the vantage of a prosperous Europe which fortunately avoided such horrors. The outcome of Gettysburg, of no importance in itself, is merely one of many such events on the reversal of which can be hung an ideal reconstruction of the twentieth century. The real subject of the essay is thus the vicissitudes of modern Europe and the possible but unlikely regeneration of the continent by means of a United Europe Association. The historical ironies coruscate; the two great British leaders, for instance, appear in reverse and more credible roles: Gladstone as a great "Conservative Empire builder," Disraeli as a powerful leader of the Radicals.[3] History, we are to infer from this experiment with "If," is queerer than fantasy.

Churchill conceded that such conjectures can be frail instruments of analysis. "If" is a two-edged sword. Events might have turned out better, or worse: "Imagination bifurcates and loses itself along the ever-multiplying paths of the labyrinth" (ATS, 14), and as history unfolds its "confusions and misfortunes, so all proportions and relations fade and change" (M, II, 996). The further one moves from the events, the more the "ifs" proliferate and uncertainty grows. A certain act "probably turned the scale and may traceably have altered the course of history. However it is always being altered by something or other" (GC, 151). If Churchill had demanded and obtained an army for Gallipoli at the beginning, there might not have been the disaster that followed, "but who shall say what would have happened instead?" Britain might have "done nothing and been confronted with diplomatic and military reactions wholly unfavorable throughout the Southern and Eastern theatre" (WC, II, 167). Nor would Britain have been undone if Germany had built before the war the submarines she built and used in 1917, as Britain would not have allowed such a development to take place. "Every set of circumstances involved every other set of circumstances. . . . Every event must be judged in fair relation to the circumstances of the time" (WC, I, 175-76). Not knowing where to draw the line, we cannot see all the ramifications of the theoretical change or decide if it would have been for the better. Besides, "allowance must be made for the intervention of the unexpected" (WC, II, 269). The inquiry into what might have happened sometimes helps us to accept what has been; this is, sadly, the best of all possible worlds. The completeness of the fall of France turned out to be "all for the best" (*SWW*, II, 221-23). Or if the kaiser, Churchill wrote in an article, had known in 1913 of what would follow, he would have gone through with his actions all the same. Hence if he often begins, "it is an interesting speculation what might have happened had . . .," the appropriate conclusion to all such conjectures is "Who shall say?" (*HESP*, IV, 70, 139).

Churchill being a memoirist and essayist no less than a chronicler, the "if" is periodically given a personal application. Any man who achieves much success and survives many encounters with death must ask himself how he got where he did, especially if he is part of a "tragic generation." Churchill emphasizes in his autobiography certain critical junctures. Thus in the entrance examination for Sandhurst, he happened to be asked the only mathematics question he was able to answer. Otherwise he might have become a preacher or tycoon, and the "whole of my life would have been altered and that would have altered a great many other lives, which in their turn, and so on" (*MEL*, 27). If we make too much of our bad luck, he warns, we should recall our equal amount of good luck and reappraise our putative bad luck, for sometimes the long-range results are surprising. When in the armored train incident he was taken prisoner, Churchill cursed his fate. "Yet this misfortune," could he have "foreseen the future," was to make his life. One cannot separate an individual event from the skein of life; a mishap may in fact be good luck in disguise, saving "one from something much worse" (*MEL*, 102).[4]

The "if" question is most thought-provoking, even devastating, as a notable reminder of the inscrutability of history and the superficiality of all human judgments. In the *River War*, Churchill noted that "Kitchener's luck" had become proverbial and that "we instinctively try to explain astonishing success. But had the [Sudan] expedition been disastrous it would have been no less easy to collect an array of opposite chances" (*RW*, I, 236). What this wise observation can mean is spelled out in his later, more mature works. In the *World Crisis* he asserted, with grim irony at the expense of politicians and generals, that an inquiry made in March, 1915, would have found many naval officers favoring the Dardanelles attack and claiming to have contributed to its initation. That had been the experience of the commission looking into the origin of the tank, a venture which succeeded and which therefore had everyone ready to be associated with it even though for a long time Churchill alone had retained faith in the idea. But the Dardanelles inquest was made in 1917, and nobody was willing to be implicated in failure.

On the other hand, had war not followed upon the crisis of July, 1914, Churchill would, for the highly praised act of sending the fleet to its war station, have been accused of endangering peace, acting without authority, increasing financial liabilities, losing his head, and manifesting another of his freaks. He would have had to defend himself before a divided cabinet and an uninstructed public opinion. So also if the experiments with the development of the tank, for which he secreted Admiralty funds, had proved abortive, he would have been vulnerable to the charge of wasting public money in a matter outside his purview and expertise. In the *Second World War* he noted the same irony: if he had been removed in 1942, as in 1915, during a government crisis and in the wake of three years of unbroken disasters, someone else would have been credited with the turn of events which began soon thereafter. How thin, in short, is the dividing line between the hero and the scapegoat. The same ingenuity, resourcefulness, and daring can bring upon one, depending on the vagaries of others or of chance, such different destinies and reputations. As he had said of a general in the Boer War: he "played for a great stake," and because he won, men easily "forget the adverse chances" (*IH*, 197). That is the major lesson of "If."

## IV   *The Theater of History*

If one problem in the writing of history is the correlation of past and present and another is the correlation of what happened and what might have, a third is the relationship of narrator to audience. Young Churchill exhibited a Victorian awareness of the reader's presence and engaged him in a dialogue of sorts. As narrator he "disarms" the criticisms of the "cantankerous" and assumes that "the reader will prefer to ride with the cavalry screen, with nothing in front of the patrols but the hostile army" (*RW*, II, 74, 76); he counsels the reader who would know what a musket barrage sounded like to "drum the fingers of both his hands on a wooden table, one after the other as quickly and as hard as he can" (*L*, 412). He begs of him forgiveness and forgetfulness; he communes with him over the proper title for the book; he pretends that the reader accompanies him, toiling "along in the dust and heat," and, therefore, "while a hundred rifles" are being unpacked, "the reader's attention" is directed to reflections on supply. If the reader has been following only in order to assail Churchill, the latter, not one to back down, rejoices "to reciprocate his detestation" (*RW*, II, 2). By the 1930s, Churchill used such locutions rarely and self-consciously: "Are you quite sure, 'gentle reader' (to revive an old-fashioned form), you would have withstood the treatment?" (*GC*, 22).

The narrator addressing his reader no less directly imposes himself on the story. Though his World War II coworkers say that, unlike most great men, he lacked "vanity," Churchill wrote eight million words, nearly all of them related in some way to himself; rarely has a writer been so self-centered. In his earliest nonfiction books, he is already a considerable presence. He comments on the work's structure or injects himself for transitions: "I desire for a moment to take a more general view," "I rejoice to record." The trivial and irrelevant often jostle the important; personal visits to Luxor and Aswân are included because they pertain to the author and bespeak his tourism and curiosity. The emotions or circumstances of the time of composition are often on display, such as his joy over his escape or over a victory. He is a busybody. He may be with the general's staff—"We. . . ." He attaches himself to a squadron of Lancers or company of Buffs to witness at the brigade level the "operations which had been ordered." He accompanies an officer into the danger zones or a political officer on diplomatic missions. The great battle of Omdurman is seen not only by the omniscient chronicler but also by the "subaltern of horse" often sent out to reconnoiter and once participating in a famous charge. He also acts; the armored train incident puts him at the center of things, where he quickly takes charge of men. In *My African Journey*, Churchill's personality—as he passes through the various places in the role of a visiting dignitary shaking hands, making speeches, opening schools, talking politics, going hunting, returning to places in the Sudan familiar from the River War—is as much on display as the exotic continent he visits.

In the *World Crisis* special attention is given, of course, to Churchill's work at his various key administrative posts in the Admiralty, at the Munitions, War, and Colonial Ministries, including his frequent extracurricular gentleman's tours of the front. Churchill's mobility in the highest circles gave him access to many important world personages, and he misses no opportunity to record such contacts, however slight. He is often seen alone with Lloyd George, conversing, debating, deciding; "he repeatedly discussed with me every aspect of the war and many of his secret hopes and fears" (*WC*, III, 262). Armistice night finds him dining with the prime minister amid, symbolically enough, portraits of British worthies.

This parading of prominent persons might be justified on the grounds of their relations to vital issues and events. Such an explanation cannot be offered for the obtrusiveness of other aspects of Churchill's life. Stray details from that personal life wander in and out of the narrative for no discernible reason other than that—again as in his early books—what happened to him, or the way in which important news reached him, is thought intrinsically of interest. Thus the historical narrative proceeds from the viewpoint of the omniscient writer when abruptly, unaccountably, the "I" intrudes. His explanation hardly suffices: "I never tire of the smallest detail. . . . They will have a definite value and an enduring interest for posterity; so I shall briefly record exactly what happened to me"(*WC*, I, 205).

In the *Second World War*, the narrator's emotions, tastes, and idiosyncrasies are again on display. Visiting during the blitz the ruins of London, he wept; seeing long queues on a cold rainy night, he wondered how long the people could endure. Various setbacks depressed him physically. Melancholy is, however, far from being the dominant chord in his personality as presented here. He seems intent on exhibiting a dappled profile of himself as a mixture of curiosity and adventurousness—which sends him often to the front lines or into air travel, sometimes on the spur of the moment, despite wartime risks—and cautious prudence, which manifests itself once he is at the front or in the air, with sober second thoughts. If he enjoys depicting the simplicity of his tastes vis-à-vis the pomp of the Communist leaders, he also avows his interest in creature comforts, and as the war situation improved and his trips abroad increased in frequency, duration, and length, a note of growing hedonism enters the narrative.

He has, moreover, little difficulty in proving to his satisfaction that nearly everyone else appreciates him as much as he does himself. His vanity expresses itself, as in the *World Crisis*, in a subtle way. Scattered through the work are letters and telegrams to its author from personages of all sorts, missives which, quoted in connection with some discussion or other, incidentally contain highly laudatory remarks. Though he often cut passages apparently not relevant, he did not always do so with the praise. Immodesty stayed his hand. George VI, Eisenhower, Smuts, Hopkins, Hull, Beaverbrook, Wallace, Stalin, even the normally critical Menzies and de Gaulle, use words like "magnificent," "savior," "glorious," "wise," "Herculean," "great," "strength" about him, for sooner or later they all seem to have come under his spell. Other personages have a way of leaving the stage of history prophesying greatness for our man. A Foreign Office official rendered prostrate by his government's flaccidity in 1936 melodramatically declares, while dying, that "Winston has always, always understood, and he is strong and will go on to the end" (*SWW*, I, 198). Words to that effect are uttered before their deaths by the French Minister Campnichi, the Italian Count Ciano, and the Anglophobic Admiral Darlan. The pages and memos devoted to Eisenhower and George VI dissuading him from participation in the Normandy invasion show that Churchill is still playing soldier in old age, dreaming of leading great armies, and, as memoirist, vain enough to dawdle over trivia.

The charge of "warmonger" had haunted him most of his life, and he had defended himself by claiming to be a man with the rare ability to both "win a war well" and "make a good peace" (*MEL*, 331). In this work, the charge is associated with one of his greatest claims to fame. Prophet—that is the role in which he always cast himself and which history at last gladly accorded him. Years before, he believed that the destruction of the coalition government in 1922 would prove chaotic; "I warned the public of what was in store. But nobody would listen."[5] His world war memoirs and many of his speeches, especially post-World War II, often echo this remark—"no one would listen," "vindicated by events." The re-

frain of the *Second World War* is, "All this was certainly borne
out by events." Postwar information and developments cor-
roborated to his satisfaction his claims about Germany in the
1930s, India and Russia in the 1940s, though at the time he
seemed alone and seemed to have finished his career by making such claims.

In Churchill's long narrative he himself is not, of course, the
only important character. He sometimes condescends to share
the stage with other individuals and nations. The resulting
tableaux are, however, awkward because he was too egocentric a writer to be proficient at character portrayal. He periodically made the attempt, with varying success. If *Malakand*
contains no clearly delineated character besides that of the
adventurer-chronicler, the *River War* manages to convey some
sense of the personality of four personages, the two pairs of
rivals—the Mahdi and Gordon, men curiously alike, and the
Khalifa Abdullahi and Kitchener, the latter a complex figure
with massive strengths and weaknesses. In the books on the
Boer War, the many failings of General Bullers are suppressed,
and the achievements of Generals Roberts and Hamilton are
rather celebrated than analyzed. The protagonist of *Randolph
Churchill* occupies a large place in the narrative, but at least a
greater attempt is made at portraying a diversity of characters
than in any book so far—Wolff, Gorst, Balfour, Salisbury,
Gladstone, Joseph Chamberlain, Northcote.

In the *World Crisis* we get little sense of the interplay of
individuals with differing personalities and philosophies.
Political and military figures enter and leave the story with
mere labels like "the Prime Minister" or "Sir John French"
attached to them. Several admirals and generals—Wilson,
Fisher, Jellicoe, Joffre, Petain, Nivelle, Haig, Von Hötzen-
dorff, Kemal, Hindenburg, Ludendorff—are, to be sure, given
brief descriptions, and two—Foch and Kitchener—are given
somewhat more detailed treatment. Of the politicians there
are brief sketches mainly of the prewar Austrian leaders and
the postwar Irish rebels. The only men who can be said to
emerge from the story with clear-cut personalities are Lloyd
George and Woodrow Wilson.

In the writings of the 1930s, Churchill was beginning to
learn something of the art. *Amid These Storms* and *Great Contemporaries* make important addenda to the sketchy portrai-

ture in the *World Crisis* with more nearly three-dimensional studies of Ludendorff, Foch, Clemenceau, and, above all, Lloyd George, as well as of individuals not mentioned in the *World Crisis*. The *Roving Commission* is filled with brief glimpses of striking Victorians who made Churchill's range of acquaintances an exciting one, whether polished aristocrats, quintessential British officers, both good and bad, imperial governors, witty journalists and intellectuals. And in *Marlborough*, for once equal to the demands of the narrative art, Churchill brings before the reader an array of diverse, fascinating characters. As in no other work of his (except possibly the *History*), he graces the characters' entry into the story with a vivid, if sometimes simplistic, "portrait" and subsequently relates their actions to their personalities or to changing circumstances. This method brings to life Harley, Godolphin, Prince Eugene, Louis XIV, James II, William III—although his tendency to think in terms of heroes and villains has subjected some of these portraits to criticism by historians. Besides the protagonist, who is analyzed at length, three persons tower over the others: the hero's wife, Sarah; his sovereign, Anne; and his main political foe, Bolingbroke.

After holding the main office in the land, Churchill, almost in spite of himself, gives in the *Second World War* sketches of his fellow leaders—Roosevelt, de Gaulle, Stalin, Hitler—and scathing observations on four Englishmen—Baldwin, Chamberlain, Wavell, Auchinleck—who, he believed, were not up to the "level of events." But this is pallid stuff, and in none of his war memoirs can the portraiture be compared with that in his works of history and biography, where the detached historian rather than the defensive participant is correlating events. Hence the *History*, like *Marlborough* and, to a degree, *Randolph Churchill* and *Contemporaries*, contains a large number of portraits of some of the interesting figures of history. Their presence follows partly from the Churchillian thesis that prominent men make history; since for once a Churchill making history is not monopolizing attention, the author can relax and be generous to other personalities. His portraits, confined exclusively at first to kings and then to politicians, also pay tribute to the builders, good and evil, of Britain, those who were first to do one thing or another. In depicting the drama of Charles I and Oliver Cromwell, his narrative powers are at their finest, evoking, as in *Marlborough*, the minutiae of religious and political controversy and creating vivid, if arguable, sketches of the two major figures and of their followers in the Civil War.

No less important than the portrayal of character is the dramatization of events and of the interplay of characters. A vivid example of young Churchill's ability to present concretely the impact on the nation of a rising political tyro is his hypothetical domestic scene in a typical middle-class household:

The worthy, pious, and substantial citizen, hurriedly turning over the pages of his *Times* and folding it to his convenience, crouched himself in his most comfortable chair and ate it up line by line with snorts of indignation or gurglings of mirth. "Look what he says about Gladstone. I wonder the *Times* prints such things. How lowering to the dignity of the public life! I can't think why they pay so much attention to this young man. Randolph Churchill, indeed – preposterous! Give me the paper back, my dear." (*RC*, I, 277)

Notwithstanding his weakness at character portrayal in the *World Crisis*, his narrative powers are to the fore in the presentation of dramatic moments: the actions of Grey, Lloyd George, and Churchill during the Agadir crisis; Grey's reading to a weary Cabinet, absorbed in the Irish question, of the Austrian ultimatum to Serbia; the opening (and closing) hours of the war; the falling out of Fisher and Churchill; the appearance of the German fleet on the high seas amid the political crisis which resulted in Churchill's dismissal; Hindenburg's entry from retirement into the Russian front, together with the rise of Ludendorff; the defeat and suicide of Samsonov, whose army of 250,000 is destroyed in a matter of days; the meteoric rise and fall of General Nivelle; the March, 1918, German offensive, and its impact on the kaiser, Ludendorff, Haig, Foch; the first entry of the American troops on the front line amid a French setback; the poignant eulogy on the dead at the Somme, a sort of "taps" in prose.

In *Marlborough*, the narrative often rises to the heights, as in the tale of the daring secret march to the Danube: "A scarlet caterpillar, upon which all eyes were at once fixed, began to crawl steadfastly day by day across the map of Europe, dragging the whole war along with it" (*M*, I, 749). Suddenly everything was thrown into uncertainty, and the French plans had to be suspended. "Massin on the Danube, Tallard on the Rhine, Villeroy on the Moselle, Bedmar on the Meuse—all stood still, waiting with strained attention upon Marlborough's movements" (*M*, I, 750). The initiative had passed to the Englishman. As he marched on, he coolly ignored Allied calls for succor from various directions. His confident estimate, not his allies' anxiety, proved correct. The army's route is only gradually unfolded by the narrator. "In the hostels of backstreets men mounted their horses and rode westward into the night along the Moselle. Ride, horseman, ride! Ride to Villeroy, to Tallard, and on to Paris, bearing news of high consequence. There will be no campaign upon the Moselle. The English have all gone higher up into Germany" (*M*, I, 755). This land odyssey, climaxed with two great victories, reads like a story within a story.

Other dramatic scenes include the government's confession to a stunned, long-silent House of incompetence in connection with the Almanzar fiasco; the first showdown of Harley with Marlborough and Godolphin, in 1707, when the Cabinet Council found itself unable to deliberate without the commander in chief and the lord treasurer (who had both resigned in protest), and a tearful queen had to accept the resignation of Harley and the return of the two "super-Ministers" she now hated. Most dramatic of all are the closing days of Anne's reign and of the body of this tale, when Bolingbroke finds himself at last at the helm, but with no time. "In the morning all the power was in his hands; in the evening, he was almost an outcast" (*M*, II, 1014). It is a storybook finish to a romantic tale.

In the *Second World War*, Churchill is very good at handling military crises, as in his description of the battles of the Graf Spee, of May, 1940, of Tobruk; the concurrent battles in Crete, Syria, the Western Desert, and Alexandria. In Churchill's hands, Stilwell's May, 1944, campaign in Burma becomes a miniature epic and the Leyte Gulf battle an intriguing ballet. Of great interest is the evocation in brief compass of tumultuous political movements and political intrigue (mainly in the first and last volumes). His skill resides in his fastening on the key issues, personalities, and dramatic junctures. Dramatic rather than insightful, for instance, is the description in brief compass, of the rise of Hitler, who outwits competing per-

sonalities and masters various power blocs in Germany. Or the
tensions of June, 1940, in Paris, as Reynaud and Weygand debate over surrender, Petain and Laval loom in the background,
a solitary, taciturn de Gaulle is singled out by the prescient
narrator-participant as the man of the future, and, later, Churchill makes the agonizing decisions over the last British air
squadrons and the destruction of the French fleet.

One of the most interesting (and amusingly described)
examples of political dissimulation is the Anglo-American de-
stroyer-bases arrangement of 1940, in which each leader tried
to allay nationalistic passions in his nation's legislature by
pointing out how the transaction served their own country's
interest better than the other country's, and the exchange was
finally presented to the world as a pair of unrelated parallel
spontaneous gestures.

In Volume 3, the negotiations among the great powers, Russia, Japan, Germany, are reduced to the essentials which make
Britain's lonely stand fearful indeed, and in volume 6 the pro-
liferating signs of Soviet perfidy and suspicion reach Churchill just as Roosevelt lapses into illness and as a paralysis
seems to grip the West. Rendered with great liveliness are the
many scenes in which he was a participant, such as the occasion of his following the battle of the *Bismarck* in the Admiralty room and at the same time reporting to the House on the
battle in Crete.

Finally there are the great scenes in which the narrator's eye
for telling detail, the evocation of setting, mood, and character
is that of a first-class novelist; for example, the one occasion on
which Molotov revealed a human side: before flying home in
1942 after signing the Anglo-Soviet treaty, "I gripped
[Molotov's] arm and we looked each other in the face. Suddenly he appeared deeply moved. Inside the image there appeared the man. He responded with an equal pressure. Silently we wrung each other's hands. But then we were all together, and it was life or death for the lot" (*SWW*, I, 369).

Compelling as literature, if somewhat deficient as history,
are the pages on the Munich crisis, with their poignant quotations from German documents and testimony, their anecdote
illustrating true honor. The narrator's piercing, even comic in-
terjections bring out the rich ironies of the confrontation between the naive, credulous democratic leaders and the deter-

mined, duplicitous Hitler. Then, as is common in this work, a single telling anecdote placed at a critical point brings out the moral meaning: a member of the French military mission in Prague resigned his citizenship and placed himself at the Czech government's disposal. The anecdote is followed by the French government's explanation that Czech concessions to the German demands had saved French honor. "We must leave this to the judgment of history" (*SWW*, I, 303), comments Churchill; but his anecdote of the general has already silently conveyed his version of true honor, his anticipation of the judgment of history.

CHAPTER 8

# *"An Affair of Sentences": Style*

## I *Weaknesses*

THAT Churchill's style is flawed, sometimes seriously so, is a recurrent criticism, the validity of which cannot be denied. His early writing tends toward redundancy and sentimentality. When he says of sleepless soldiers that "insulted nature asserted itself" and they drifted into the "peaceful unconsciousness of utter exhaustion" (*MFF*, 102), the adjectives bloat the style: "insulted," like the verb "asserted," is a pathetic fallacy, while "peaceful" and "utter" contribute little. He speaks melodramatically of the "spurts of dust" from bullets on all sides showing "where Fate is stepping" (*MFF*, 299). Even in old age, purple passages came a little too easily to him: "I turn from the pink and ochre panorama of Athens and Piraeus, scintillating with delicious life and plumed by the classic glories and endless miseries and triumphs of its history" (*Vi*, 22). To speak of a cruiser sunk off the west coast of Australia with all seven hundred men lost as "a sombre sacrifice in lonely waters" (*SWW*, III, 521) is to let the adjectives give the sentence a Victorian portentousness. In a famous passage from his speech on the Munich crisis—the government "go on in strange paradox, decided only to be undecided, resolved to be irresolute, adamant for drift, solid for fluidity, all powerful to be impotent" (*WES*, 326)—the first part of the sentence is effective, but "resolved" and "irresolute" repeat "decided" and "undecided"; "solid" and "fluidity" repeat "adamant" and "drift." By the time he reaches "all powerful," the reader realizes that these two words mean nothing at all; Churchill has repeated the oxymoron too often.

Churchill may, as when contrasting in the *World Crisis* the outwardly peaceful world with the one ready to leap into being—a "world of monstrous shadows moving in convulsive combinations through vistas of fathomless catastrophe" (*WC*, I, 18)–indulge in terrible overwriting. That work also contains melodramatic tableaux: General Nivelle plans an offensive and "behind him stood Colonel D'Alençon with fevered eye and a year to live. At his side was the redoubtable Mangin burning with the ardour of battle" (*WC*, III, 286). Or on the Russian Revolution: "And behind all, cold, calculating, ruthless, patient, stirring all, demanding all, awaiting all, the world-wide organization of International Communism" (*WC*, VI, 378). The plight of the czar brings out the most maudlin in Churchill: "He is about to be struck down. A dark hand, gloved at first in folly, now intervenes. Exit Czar. . . . Nicholas II, casting his eyes now towards the Providence he sought to serve, now towards the family group he loved so well, clung chained to his post" (*WC*, III, 229; VI, 377). When he does not like someone, nearly every word expresses his contempt, and invective displaces analysis, understanding, fairness: Gandhi was "a malignant subversive fanatic," "a seditious Middle-Temple lawyer, now posing as a fakir, striding half-naked" (*Ind*, 94-95).

From his early reading in Gibbon and Macaulay came a certain *copia* and patterning that is variously cloying, predictable, archaic, or rhetorical. That he learned to model his parallelisms and antitheses on theirs is all too clear in some early, factitious examples: "The philosopher may observe with pity and the philanthropist deplore with pain" (*MFF*, 301). Some of the influence lingers in *Randolph Churchill*: "The frowns of age and authority melted at his advance, and rebuke and envy pursued him idly" (*RC*, II, 296); and even in a speech in old age: "Miseries and humiliations beyond the power of statistics to measure or language to describe" (*EU*, 436).

Then there is the problem of the superlative. In his early unpublished essay, "The Scaffolding of Rhetoric," Churchill listed five ingredients for great oratory, the last of which was extravagance and exaggeration. This device was still common in the writings of the mature man. He himself, in fact, as he said of one of his fictional characters, "always lived in the superlative" (*S*, 62). Though he admitted during World War II that "it has become a hackneyed phrase to say 'never been surpassed,'" he kept on saying it (*DoL*, 260). The man who believed that "ramming a point home" by iteration is a justified appeal to the "common sense and conscience of the nation" was not likely to underestimate superlatives (*EU*, 307). The extent to which Churchill sometimes literally compared things is indicated by his qualification of one of the superlatives, "So rapid an advance by such powerful forces over distances so enormous is without parallel in modern war; and the Ancients had not the advantages of locomotion which we possess, so they are out of it anyway" (*OtV*, 32).

While some legitimately bring unusual matters to our attention, other superlatives had only a transient significance and were soon to be eclipsed, as a result of technological progress and the growth in the world's population. The events and statistics of one war tend, at least in modern times, to be displaced by those of the next war, for, as Churchill says in another connection, "modern technical conditions have been given so great an extension ... that comparisons with other times are vitiated" (*WC*, V, 120). Yet other superlatives seem trivial, irrelevant, or poor attempts at humor. They are rhetorical gestures, attempts to elevate trivia or the result of lack of perspective. And many, by far the majority, are plainly arguable or blatantly false, such as the contention that the Egyptian army of 1883 was "perhaps the worst that has ever marched to war" (*RW*, I, 52), that Lend Lease "must be regarded without question as the most unsordid act in the whole of recorded history" (*US*, 286), that Titus Oates was as "wicked as any man who ever lived" (*HESP*, II, 279).

Churchill can make such wild assertions because comparisons are difficult and scientific precision is not in question. They quickly pall, however, like tired metaphors. They are used in the common colloquial manner of exaggerating to make a point, to express intensity or extremity. When he says, for instance, that in 1940 he presented to the House the shortest and most popular program in history, he is merely using the superlative to say that all Britons were of one mind. Sometimes such a nebulous or disputable sort of assertion is allied with, or created by, Macaulayan antithesis: Europe is "the greatest of continents fallen into the worst of misery" (*ItB*, 83).

Churchill simply vitiates his style by overusing this device. In all his books hardly anything happens that is not the biggest and worst and best ever. The state of mind which prompts politicians in democracies to speak always of the current election campaign as the most critical in the nation's history is to be found in extreme form in him. He makes everything ride on whatever issue he fights for, turning the matter into a battle and a crisis, into a watershed of history, a matter of life or death. Whether this worship of the biggest, best, and greatest, comes from the Americaphiliac side of his personality or is an expression of his vanity is hard to say. It certainly is a form of self-glorification, of dressing up one's experience, era, or narrative, for it places oneself at the supposed greatest moment in history, confronting the greatest adversity, and makes one's emerging victorious that much more formidable. It accentuates Churchill's role at the center of the story and of the world, as though all history were merely a preparation for him.

## II  Strengths: Imagery and Humor

In his autobiography, Churchill boasted of often noticing "deep resemblances between many different kinds of things" (*MEL*, 212). This is no idle claim, and if, as some literary critics hold, the ability to correlate disparate entities is at the heart of the poetic process, Churchill is, in his fashion, a prose poet. Thoough not usually as striking as Shakespeare's or Milton's, his similes and metaphors vivify his discourse and clarify his meaning.

Some of his images are conventional animal emblems for various nations; lions, bears, tigers, crocodiles, and vultures abound. Equally numerous and effective are references to seas, tides, and currents in discussions of movements, tendencies, and events; swimmers and ships stand for individuals, classes, nations. Storms, seasonal changes, weather, and atmospheric conditions are likewise common. Political matters are often visualized in terms of abysses, heights, broadness, and light or sunniness.

No less comprehensive, flexible, and perceptive is Churchill's use of imagery from the institutions of society and the disciplines of man – from Scripture, marriage, commerce, science, medicine, sports, games, painting, and, especially, the theater. By far the richest source of imagery was the discipline which had been Churchill's first vocation and thereafter remained his avocation, soldiering. He often saw life, notably life in the limelight, as a "battlefield." In discussing the need for social reform, the young Churchill justified his use of an

extended military metaphor by citing six years' experience as
a soldier, and in later years he even confessed to being "always twitted with using warlike metaphors"; his defense was
that he had been in contact with many wars and that now the
whole world had grown familiar with military matters.[1]

While some of his metaphors and similes are predictable or
pedestrian, others are effectively, even pithily, used. Churchill adeptly moves, for instance, from the literal to the figurative when speaking of free trade: the world's shipping comes
to Britain because "our harbors are more nearly as nature
made them," not being obstructed with "fiscal stake nets and
tariff mud bars" (*FFT*, 57). Or he may fuse the literal to the
figurative as when he uses "windows" to stand for documents,
historical evidence. Thus in one powerful sentence—"Upon
this [medieval] darkness we have four windows, each
obstructed by dim or colored glass" (*HESP*, I, 41)—the image
is evocative, for the word "colored" applies to the stained
glass of medieval churches, therefore to dogma and by extension to events distorted or obscured by religious chroniclers.
And some images, in themselves trivial, form complex patterns in individual works. Of such a nature is staring or gazing
in the *History*, sounds and silence in the *World Crisis*, and
sleep in the *Second World War*.

Even more interesting, or at least more famous, than his imagery is Churchill's humor. His writings are pervaded by a
sense of the comic dimension rare among either politicians or
historians, who are normally custodians of the solemn. Churchill not only kept his eye cocked for comical incidents but
also often made modifiers and phrases introduce comic overtones to situations which without his intervention would not
strike most people as incongruous. He achieved humorous effects either by deliberately accumulating phrases or with a
sudden sharp thrust of a single word. Many of his witticisms
are rooted in his command of a wide vocabulary and an
orotund style. He sometimes handles even trivialities in a portentous, polysyllabic manner which aims not at impressing but
at amusing. Thus the discrepancy between men's creeds and
actions is underlined by avoidance of the commonplace and
therefore lifeless word "Christmas" in narrating the Irish Parliament's debate over the Treaty of 1922: "They adjourned at
length to celebrate the nativity of the Saviour, and when they
resumed in January they were cleft in twain" (*WC*, V, 324). Wit

may express itself as much through the single word, commonly an adjective or adverb, as through intentional ponderousness: thus a slave trader is described as protesting "with superfluous energy that he was no saint" (*RW*, I, 44). Sometimes even a mere syllable, a prefix, gives an unexpected and therefore amusing twist to a conventional utterance: it nicely conveys, for example, the political nature of the French appointment of General Sarrail: "Whatever dispute there might be about his military achievements, his irreligious convictions were above suspicion" (*WC*, II, 491).

One effective type of wordplay is the zeugma, the use of words in parallel grammatical, but not logical, form: a wirenetted cube at the El Alamein position was "full of flies and important military personages" (*SWW*, IV, 458). Closely related to zeugma are parallelism and antithesis. Besieged troops were in difficulty when they "began to eat instead of feed the horses" (*L*, 487).

Much of Churchill's humor is dependent on the manipulation not merely of words but also of logic and perspective. And just as extremes of wordiness or of the single word may be amusing, so may the extremes of understatement and hyperbole. In abolishing the original decision to use church-bell warnings of an invasion, he noted that it was a redundant method because "I cannot help feeling that anything like a serious invasion would be bound to leak out" (*OtV*, 107). But Churchill could also incite laughter by resorting to the opposite device—of hyperbole, or exaggeration rather than understatement. Hence in the following sentence, the nouns undermine the ensuing, climactic adjective: "That is one of those glimpses of the obvious and the obsolete with which his powerful speech abounded" (*US*, 122). A special form of hyperbole is the *reductio ad absurdum*, the parody of someone's logic. When the press spoke of the cession to Ireland of all rights to the Irish ports as a release from Britain's "onerous and delicate task of defending" the ports, Churchill commented, "Further releases might have been obtained by handing over Gibraltar to Spain and Malta to Italy" (*SWW*, I, 278).

### III   *Strengths: Words, Phrases, Sentences*

Churchill's style contains, as is well known, a profusion of Latinate, polysyllabic words, as in the sally, "the half under-

stood vocabulary of irritated ignorance" (*LSP*, 390). Such
words can be effective not only in themselves but also in a
tension or contrast with the other great reservoir of English
vocabulary. In a selection about a modern general's life—it
holds "no anodyne of danger, relief in violent action; nothing
but anxiety, suspense, perplexing and contradictory information; weighing the imponderable, assigning proportions to
what cannot be measured, intricate staff duties, difficult personal negotiations, and the mutterings of far-distant guns"
(*GC*, 195)—the formal Latinate language is climaxed with
Anglo-Saxon words (curiously echoing the rhythm of Tennyson's renowned "murmuring of innumerable bees") repre-
senting the one sensuous contact with ominous reality, the one
concrete fact in a life filled with paperwork and abstractions.
In the following excerpt from a wartime speech, each sentence
contains at least one "literary" word and the last one closes
with a reminder of past greatness in a run of monosyllables
climaxed by the dying fall of the drawn-out "all" and the disyl-
labic "a-lone": "Let us go, then, to battle on every front.
Thrust forward every man who can be found. Arm and equip
the forces in bountiful supply. Listen to no parley from the
enemy. Vie with our valiant allies to intensify the conflict.
Bear with unflinching fortitude whatever evils and blows we
may receive. Drive on through the storm, now that it reaches
its fury, with the same singleness of purpose and inflexibility
of resolve as we showed to the world when we were all alone"
(*DoL*, 165).

    Conscious of levels of usage, Churchill enjoys racy col-
loquialisms no less than formal Latinisms: a mayor urged the
"Government to get a move on—though he may have used a
more ceremonious expression" (*UA*, 192). His informality
produced, in formal speeches, phrases like "there are quite a
lot of us to be killed," "let them stew in their own juices," "see
what is in the cupboard," or sentences like "I would have
pulled them to pieces the other way round" and "the quarrel
could be put right if only they could talk things over" (*EU*,
329, 333). Admiral Jellicoe's failures are dismissed with a
terse, withering colloquial sentence: "Three times is a lot"
(*WC*, III, 159). Sometimes, as when deglamorizing war, Churchill mingles the literary word ("conflict," "ruffian") with the
earthy ("bash," "snout," "something better"): "Alas, I must

write it: the actual conflict had to be more like one ruffian bashing the other on the snout with a club, a hammer, or something better" (*SWW*, I, 587). Churchill effectively demolishes the Lords' pretension to detachment and impartiality by a thorough shift from the Latinate, the literary, the "ideal," to the proverbial, the colloquial, the sordidly "real": "Beneath the imposing mask of an assembly of notables braced by the prescription and tradition of centuries we discern the leer of the artful dodger, who has got the straight tip from the party agent" (*LSP*, 217). Instead of saying something politically conventional and decorous like "the Germans tyrannize over countries they conquer," Churchill resorts to the lively "the Germans have a way when they get into countries of throwing their weight about" (*SbS*, 308). No other major statesman who could be eloquent made such use of colloquialisms. In a wartime speech he referred to nascent Anglo-American cooperation in August, 1940, as getting "mixed up together" (*BST*, 351). He especially resorted to colloquialisms in speeches or articles addressed to America: "I should have hesitated a long time before getting mixed up with Europe and Asia and that sort of thing."[2] And many of his most famous sentences—"Never . . . ," "Give us the tools . . . ," "Do your worst . . . ," "We shall fight . . ."—consist if not of colloquialisms at least of the simplest of words.

Churchill was as adept with logical sequences as with levels of usage. Indeed, one brief passage unfolds like a syllogism: "Murder is rare. But murder is punished, and perhaps it is because murder is punished that it is rare" (*PR*, 142). Epigrammatic statements are often forged by means of balance: "War is made with steel, and steel is made with coal" (*EoB*, 253); "Private soldiers do not give their lives as easily as dictators make speeches" (*SbS*, 95); "Neither Haig's view of Lloyd George nor Lloyd George's view of Haig is likely to be accepted by history. They will both be deemed much better men than they deemed each other" (*GC*, 196). In

|   |   |   |   |
|---|---|---|---|
| A | B | B | A |

" 'War is hell,' he [Sherman] said, and certainly he made it so" (*HESP*, IV, 199)

the effect is created by the symmetry around the pivotal word "certainly" and the significant alteration from "said" to "made."

The sequence of words and phrases may underline an antithesis. In the following sentences—"The inherent vice of capitalism is the unequal sharing of blessings. The inherent virtue of Socialism is the equal sharing of miseries" (*SoP*, 23)—the antithesis makes the worst of the one seem better than the best of the other. A lifetime's preoccupation with the right and the wrong time to give, with the advantages and disadvantages of giving, battle decorations, resulted in the laconic, "A metal glitters, but it also casts a shadow" (*DoL*, 28). The antithesis may be given added thrust by wordplay: "The production of new wealth must precede [the Socialists'] common wealth, otherwise there will only be common poverty" (*Vi*, 305); "Before they nationalized our industries they should have nationalized themselves. [The new sense of "nationalized" immediately follows.] They should have set country before party" (*EU*, 27).

Another Churchillian device is the series of four words, either adjectives or nouns. Winston Weathers theorizes that the leader speaks to the emotions with a four-or-more-part series because a triad like "blood, sweat, and tears" is too ordinary and "blood and tears" is too definite and complete, lacking any sense of sacrifices still to be made.[3] This hypothesis may or may not persuade, but the fact is that Churchill used the device throughout his career. It appears often in connection with some form of combat, as in a speech during the battle with the Lords over the 1909 People's Budget: "That is the whole policy of His Majesty's Government—blunt, sober, obvious, and unflinching" (*LSP*, 404). In the *World Crisis*, he wrote apropos the Dardanelles, "As yet all was unconscious, inchoate, purposeless, uncombined" (*WC*, I, 545). Just before World War II, he struck the elegiac note: "All is over. Silent, mournful, abandoned, broken, Czechoslovakia recedes into the darkness" (*BST*, 58). And after the famous series of 1940, he reverted to the device, as in his remarks that he "never brooded over a situation" demanding "more patience, composure, courage, and perseverance" (*UA*, 147).

Effects may be achieved with one or two modifiers alone. A siege undertaken reluctantly by Marlborough, who prefers open battles, is "local and stony fare" (*M*, II, 570). When Churchill says that the successful secret jamming of the German navigational beam caused the "very few who knew" to exchange "celestial grins" (*SWW*, II, 387), "celestial" suggests a silent secret victory, the joy of outwitting someone cunning, and the locale of the victory, the sky. Research on a photoelectric fuse resulted in a model Churchill could show to the Cabinet, "but there is a long road between a grimacing model and an armed mass-production robot" (*SWW*, II, 396); the ominousness in the adjective "grimacing" is fulfilled in the noun and climactic word, "robot." In speaking of alternative military operations if it proved impossible to help the mainland Greek forces, Churchill concluded, "But these will only be consolation prizes after the classic race has been lost" (*SWW*, III, 66). "Classic" not only means "basic" or "major" but connotes classical, Greece, olympic game contests, Marathon, battles for freedom. In one sentence – the retired and ill Pitt drilled with a "motley company of yokels on the fields of the South Coast, while a bare twenty miles away across the Channel the Grand Army of Napoleon waited only for a fair wind and clear passage" (*HESP*, III, 243) – the danger Britons of all classes faced and overcame is rendered with vividness and pride by a dramatic juxtaposition, helped by the frightening "only" and the opposing associations of "motley, yokels" and "Grand Army, Napoleon." (Compare "The days when the Spanish Armada was approaching the Channel, and Drake was finishing his game of bowls" [*BST*, 368].

A single detail sharply distinguishes medieval from modern life: "Every district had a life of its own and very few lights burned after sundown" (*HESP*, I, 232). The homely detail may bring out the contrast between the "official" or ideal and the personal, quotidian sides of man: "On one day there was a Parliament regarding itself as the responsible custodian of national destiny, ready to embark upon dire contention; the next a jumble of Members scrambling for conveyances to carry them home" (*HESP*, II, 290). Or conversely, a rapid change from concreteness to generalization startles the reader: in the deceptively casual remark that after Gettysburg, Lee managed to get his army across a river, having "lost only two guns, and the war" (*HESP*, IV, 185), a minor detail illustrating the tactical and logistical triumph (undoubtedly appreciated by Lee

and his staff) of crossing the river with slight losses is juxtaposed with a vast adverse abstract significance apparent
only to the historian and his reader. These three simplest of
words ("and the war"), seeming to come almost as an after-
thought, an appendage to the sentence, are part of a tremendous zeugma, which dramatizes a modification of the concept
of Pyhrric victory, a reversal of deGaulle's famous remark
about France having lost a battle but not the war.

If in the attack on Gandhi, his intelligence was blunted by
his distaste, Churchill at other times could express contempt
with subtlety: The United Nations Organization is "Babel,
tempered by skilful lobbying" (*SWW*, VI, 610); "Babel" conjures up the poetic biblical, mythical, eternally recurring;
"lobbying" suggests modern prosaic democratic ways; "tempered" and "skilful" imply improvements on the biblical
Babel as part of the alleged progress which most people believe in and which Churchill has expressed his doubts about
in many of his later books. The absence of true progress is
signaled also by the decline in the art of war, a decline delineated by colored and carefully selected contrasting words:
"Instead of a small number of well-trained professionals
championing their country's cause with ancient weapons and
a beautiful intricacy of archaic maneuvers," war is now handled by "chemists in spectacles and chauffeurs pulling the lev-
ers of aeroplanes or machine guns," with "blear-eyed clerks"
to add up the "butcher's bill"; a matter of "men, money and
machinery," it is no longer a "gentleman's game" (*MEL*, 64-
66).

A pithy sentence may round out a train of thought. Richard
I's character is beautifully etched: "His life was one magnificent parade, which, when ended, left only an empty plain"
(*HESP*, I, 169). Such sentences, full of irony and resonance,
appear at the end of paragraph, section, chapter, or even volume. They galvanize the iron filings of fact into a meaningful
pattern: "The Corporal [Hitler] had traveled far" (*SWW*, I, 60);
"Facts are better than dreams" (*SWW*, I, 667); "The battle of
attrition began. Attrition! But whose?" (*SWW*, II, 338); "The
hinge had turned" (*SWW*, IV, 831). In lieu of a pithy sentence,
a telling quotation may end a section, such as Hitler's remark
after the Munich Pact: "This is the last territorial claim I have
to make in Europe" (*SWW*, I, 308), or Chamberlain's "Peace

with honor. I believe it is peace in our time" (*SWW*, I, 318), or Louis XIV's "The affair of [Bolingbroke's] displacing the Duke of Marlborough will do all for us we desire" (*M*, II, 913).

Churchill has many fine short passages in which he keeps his eye on the object, on what it signified or on how it appeared to the observer. In the *River War*, he speaks of the odyssey of the railroad workers across the "smooth ocean" of African sand, connected to the "living world of man and ideas by two parallel iron streaks, three feet six inches apart." Each morning, "with a whistle and clatter, amid the aching silence of the ages," the supply train arrived. When it left, it vanished "along a line which appeared at last to turn up into the air and run at a tangent into an unreal world" (*RW*, I, 290-91). In some passages, especially when dealing with military men, the tone is dramatic, perhaps even, as in the last sentence of the following, too nearly Hollywoodian to some tastes: in 1708, with London full of political intrigues, "Marlborough, at grips with a superior French army, worn and wearied, ill and fevered, was . . . roused after a brief collapse to the mood of Napoleon before Wagram; '*la bataille repondra.*' He cast political intrigue from him with inexpressible loathing. He left the Queen's letters unanswered, and mounted his horse" (*M*, II, 328). In this passage, as in the one above about modern generals and the following one, a series of abstractions and generalizations is capped with a concrete detail which dramatizes the basic idea and brings us down to the level of action and events. "Napoleon's Empire, with all its faults, and all its glories, fell, and flashed away like snow at Easter till nothing remained but his Majesty's ship *Bellerophon*, which awaited its suppliant refugee" (*US*, 123). Enroute to the concrete detail, we move in this sentence from worldly grandeur (the associations of the names "Napoleon" and "Empire") to an image of transience, to the proud reference to the writer's nation, whose empire, by implied contrast, abides.

A political crisis in a democracy is turned by style into a battle of Titans witnessed by awed Lilliputian M.P.'s, who can but ratify the results: "Here we see Mr. Lloyd George advancing to his goal, now with smooth and dexterous artifice, now with headlong charge. We see Mr. Asquith at bay. . . . Parliament listened bewildered to the muffled sounds of conflict proceeding behind closed doors and dutifully acclaimed the

victor who emerged" (*GC*, 124-25). One passage contains
parallel sentence structures (with the asymmetrical, climactic
"few") and the gradual introduction of evocative proper
nouns: "No one in Europe imagined the drama of terrific war
which the year 1862 would unfold. None appraised truly the
implacable rage of the antagonists. None understood the
strength of Abraham Lincoln or the resources of the U.S. Few
outside the Confederacy had ever heard of Lee or Jackson"
(*HESP*, IV, 140). Using laconic indirect dialogue in place of
the abstract summary usual with historians, he avoids the
scholar's lengthy quoting, or the popularizer's fabricating of
speeches: When Henry VIII inquired of a convocation
whether his remarriage was legal and moral, "Answer by the
prelates and clergy present: Yes. By Bishop Fisher of Roches-
ter: No. Was Prince Arthur's marriage with Queen Catherine
consummated? Answer by the clergy: Yes. By the Bishop: No.
Thereupon the Bishop was arrested and committed to the Tower" (*HESP*, II, 48). This vignette sketches the sycophancy of
the clergy, the loneliness of the man of conscience, and the
arbitrariness of an autocrat who brooks no dissent and wastes
no time.

## IV   *Strengths: Longer Passages*

Churchill was able to bring his powers to bear on extended
passages as well as on individual phrases and sentences. His
style at the very beginning of his career evinced maturity and
a way with words. In his first book, observing the "shapeless
forms coffined in a regulation blanket," he regarded "the
pride of race, the pomp of empire, the glory of war as the faint
and unsubstantial fabric of a dream; and I could not help
realizing with Burke: 'What shadows we are and what
shadows we pursue' " (*MFF*, 206). This looking-at-things-
under-the-aspect-of-eternity passage is a little too pat and
"literary"; it is composition according to the formulas of
Ecclesiastes and baroque sermons, with an obligatory reference to Burke. What would be weak in a practised writer,
however, has its charms coming from a young officer-corre-
spondent.

He may also be reaching too readily for the significant, the
comprehensive, the portentous in his description of the cul-

tural gap between the tribesmen and Western civilization: " 'Kill these,' [the tribes] had said, 'and all is done.' What did they know of the distant regiments which the telegraph wires were drawing, from far down in the south of India? Little did they realize that they had set the world humming; that military officers were hurrying 7,000 miles by sea and land from England, to the camps in the mountains; that long trains were carrying ammunition and supplies from distant depots to the front; that astute financiers were considering how their action had affected the ratio between silver and gold" or that politicians wondered as to the impact on by-elections. "These ignorant tribesmen had no conception of the sensitiveness of that modern civilization, which thrills and quivers in every part of its vast and complex system at the slightest touch. They only saw the forts and camps on the Malakand Pass" (*MFF*, 110). Yet, despite this expansiveness and leisureliness, despite the constructions of a Victorian Gibbon, he can, when disciplined by the new war journalism, describe violent action (notably in *Malakand*) with short sentences in the manner of (albeit twenty years before) Hemingway: "The fire became severe. Numerous casualties occurred. A retirement was ordered. As is usual in Asiatic warfare, it was considerably pressed. . . . The darkness fell swiftly. The smoke puffs became fire flashes. Great clouds overspread the valley and thunder began to roll. The daylight died away" (*MFF*, 132, 195).

In *Randolph Churchill* and especially in the various works of the 1920s and 1930s, he is capable of subtler effects. The *World Crisis* contains, in addition to not a few purple passages, numerous moving lines, such as the lyric effusion on the corpses moldering on the barbed wire between the trenches. In an essay of this period, recollections of his observation of the 1909 German army maneuvers in the light of subsequent history begets an elegy, an under-the-aspect-of-eternity passage in which poignance wrestles with verbosity:

Indeed, these Wurzburg manoeuvres make in my mind the picture of a Belshazzar feast. Upon how many of those who marched and cantered in that autumn sunlight had the dark angel set his seal! Violent untimely death, ruin and humiliation worse than death, privation, mutilation, despair to the simple soldier, the downfall of their pride and subsistence to the chiefs: such were the fates—could we but have read them—which brooded over thousands and tens of thousands of these virile figures. All the Kings and Princes of Germany, all the Generals of her Empire, clustered round the banqueting-tables. Ten years were to see them scattered, exiled, deposed, in penury, in obloquy—the victims of a fatal system in which they were inextricably involved. (*ATS*, 82)

Less theatrical and more thoughtful are his ruminations on one man's death. He at one point quoted approvingly Roseberry's remark, "if this is Death it is absolutely nothing," but elsewhere he went beyond such cant to the essence of the pain men feel: "As I observed [Balfour] regarding with calm, firm and cheerful gaze the approach of Death, I felt how foolish the Stoics were to make such a fuss about an event so natural and so indispensable to mankind. But I felt also the tragedy which robs the world of all the wisdom and treasure gathered in a great man's life and experience, and hands the lamp to some impetuous and untutored stripling, or lets it fall shivered into fragments upon the ground" (*GC*, 221).

He also has, however, the light touch, as in his narration of his first assay at painting:

Having bought the colors, an easel, and a canvas, the next step was to begin. But what a step to take! The palette gleamed with beads of colour; fair and white rose the canvas; the empty brush hung poised, heavy with destiny, irresolute in the air. My hand seemed arrested by a silent veto. But after all the sky on this occasion was unquestionably blue, and a pale blue at that. There could be no doubt that blue paint mixed with white should be put on the top part of the canvas. One really does not need to have had an artist's training to see that. It is a starting-point open to all. So very gingerly I mixed a little blue paint on the palette with a very small brush, and then with infinite precaution made a mark about as big as a bean upon the affronted snow-white shield. [Just then a lady-friend appeared and made] fierce strokes and slashes of blue on the absolutely cowering canvas. Anyone could see that it could not hit back. No evil fate avenged the jaunty violence. The canvas grinned in helplessness before me. The spell was broken. The sickly inhibitions rolled away. I seized the largest brush and fell upon my victim with berserk fury. I have never felt any awe of a canvas since. (*ATS*, 307)

In the autobiography, he bypasses adult habituation to the ways of mathematical numbers and recaptures the child's puzzlement over relations that seem arbitrary: "The figures were tied into all sorts of tangles and did things to one another which it was extremely difficult to forecast with complete accuracy. You had to say what they did each time they were tied up together, and the Governess apparently attached enormous importance to the answer being exact" (*MEL,* 3).

In *Marlborough,* as in his other post-World War I works, his irony pricks the modern smugness about progress and superior life-style. In evoking the earlier mode of life, he speaks of our own "happy and enlightened age, securely established upon the rock of purity and virtue, ceaselessly cleansed by the strong tides of universal suffrage," able to show tolerance and indulgence "towards the weakness and vices of those vanished generations without in any way compromising our own integrity." This Gulliverian rhetoric is suddenly disabled by an unequivocal assertion: "It is strange indeed that such a [premodern] system should have produced a succession of greater captains and abler statesmen than all our widely extended education, competitive examinations, and democratic systems have put forth" (*M,* I, 40). Irony of statement has been transformed into irony of fact.

Churchill achieves in the same work sustained poetic effects when the language of war and diplomacy describes, by contrast and by way of summary, the old warrior-diplomat amid his long yearned-for calm in retirement: "He devoted to the conciliation of domestic broils those resources of tact and patience which had so long held the confederacy of Europe united. From the habitable wing at Blenheim he watched the masonry rising up with that daily interest which had in bygone years measured so many processes of battering down; and the distant chink and clang of the hammers took the place of the cannonade by which more than thirty of the strongest fortresses in Europe had been infallibly reduced to surrender." Then Churchill reaches for the baroque rhythms of Sir Thomas Browne: "The span of mortals is short, the end universal; and the tinge of melancholy which accompanies decline and retirement is in itself an anodyne. It is foolish to waste lamentations upon the closing phase of life. Noble spirits yield themselves willingly to the successively falling shades which carry them to a better world or to oblivion." The narrator now conjures up, in the manner of that seventeenth-century writer, fa-

mous examples of warriors dying in battle or command, "with
great causes in dispute and strong action surging round; like
Charles XI at Frederickshald, like Berwick at Philipsburg, or
Wolfe on the Heights of Abraham, or Nelson at Trafalgar. But
these swift exits are not in human choice. Great captains must
take their chances with the rest. Caesar was assassinated by
his dearest friend. Hannibal was cut off by poison. Frederick
the Great lingered out years of loneliness in body and soul.
Napoleon rotted at St. Helena. Compared with these,
Marlborough had a good and fair end to his life" (*M*, II, 1035-
37).

In the *History*, rhetoric and meaning unfold magisterially in
long paragraphs, like the one describing a Roman Briton awak-
ening  in the present, or the change from Roman Britain to
England and the coming of Christianity, or the fall of
feudalism in the face of gunpowder. Subtle is the mixture of
coyness, of caution, defiance, and hope, in his description, in
one of his wartime speeches, of the first tentative joint moves
by America and Britain: "I do not view the process with any
misgivings. I could not stop it if I wished; no one can stop it.
Like the Mississippi, it just keeps rolling along. Let it roll."
Then he moves from feigned impotence and resignation to ac-
ceptance and celebration, to a widening of the horizon at the
close of passage and speech: "Let it roll on full flood, inexorable, irresistible, benignant, to broader lands and better days"
(*BST*, 351).

Churchill is usually associated with a lush, even fustian and
windy rhetoric. This is an oversimplification. There are many
Churchills—young, middle aged, old; journalist, orator, admin-
istrator, memoirist, essayist, historian—and they do not write
in the same way. There may be a multiplicity of styles in one
work, as can be seen in the *Roving Commission*, where the
supple and varied narrative can suggest the viewpoint of a
child, a Pathan tribesman, a gentleman cadet, a Victorian general or nobleman. The narrator can forge a lively apostrophe,
anecdote, or essay, or he can paint brief moving scenes of the
boy with his father or of his own last meeting with Botha. That
his style varied also with the period of his life is made clear by
the contrast, at the beginning of the *Second World War*, between excerpts from his writings of the 1920s and the later
prose in which they are set. The older passages have a certain

poetic feeling, but they also labor with Victorian personifica-
tions, melodrama, sentimentality.

Churchill's style may vary in a third way; it may be shaped
by genre and occasion. Besides the brief selections in the
older manner, the *Second World War* contains four styles. The
ample selections from his speeches are sometimes colloquial
but more often given to rich imagery, irony, and complicated
patterns of organization. Their tone is hortatory or didactic.
The strategic, administrative, and diplomatic memoranda may
be written in a formal, impersonal (for Churchill) manner, with
carefully marshaled logic and little imagery or humor; they are
as much inquisitive as didactic, for writer and addressee seek
solutions jointly. Or they may be in an informal, personal
manner, rife with satiric sallies, colloquialisms, entreaties,
good humor, or anger. Then there is the narrative style, partak-
ing at times of all these attributes. Though it can be puerile or
pedestrian, it is normally flexible, radiating, by turns, regret,
pity, joy, defensiveness, and indulgent humor and confidence.
It is the metallic foil, not unattractive in itself, in which are set
the nuggets that are individual orations and memos, for many
of the most memorable passages and phrases appear in speech
and memorandum.

There are large effects, like the two hundred word periodic
sentence which closes chapter 5, the first part of which sentence reviews the errors of the British and the smaller second
part (with its relative clauses piled on relative clauses and its
parallelisms) conveys the judgment. Such a summary sentence
usually comes after an extended narration of events. An ex-
cited passage in which short sentences come together and part
in quickly changing patterns amid a burst of lyric effusion consists of two paragraphs describing Churchill's reactions to
Pearl Harbor.

Style is, of course, more a matter of individual taste than of
objective, verifiable standards. There exists no consensus on
the subject, and if there are many Churchill styles there are
also many readers. Most moderns like their style lean and will
find the following passage (in which I number the sentences
and italicize possible redundancies) illustrative of Churchill's
weaknesses no less than of his strengths:

[1] Another conflict was going on *step by step, month by month.* [2]

This was a secret war, whose battles were lost or won unknown to the public, and only with difficulty comprehended even now, *to those outside the small high scientific circles concerned.* [3] No such warfare had ever been waged by *mortal* men. [4] The terms in which it could be recorded or talked about were unintelligible to *ordinary folk.* [5] Yet if we had not mastered its profound meaning and used its mysteries even while we *saw them only in the glimpse, all the efforts,* all the prowess of the fighting airmen, all the bravery and sacrifices of the people, would have been in vain. [6] Unless British science had proved superior to German, and unless its *strange sinister* resources had been effectively brought to bear on the struggle *for survival,* we might well have been defeated, and, *being defeated,* destroyed. (*SWW,* II, 381)

This is good writing but somewhat overdone. The second sentence takes too long to tell us of the secrecy of the war; in the following sentence, "mortal" is Victorian window dressing. In sentence 4, which repeats the idea conveyed by the last half of 2, "ordinary folk" is condescending. The fifth and last sentences are again too long; "strange sinister" iterates the point made earlier by "secret," "with difficulty comprehended," "unintelligible," "mysteries"; and "destroyed" makes "for survival" unnecessary. Those who like an ornate style, however, will dismiss these objections as the carping of a narrowly conceived modern functionalism.

But there can be no difference of opinion over the merits of the majestic sentence near the close of volume 1 (which I print in this fashion in order to exhibit its structure):

      [1]    Thus, then,
                  on the night of the tenth of May,
                  at the outset of this mighty battle,
[2]   I acquired the chief power in the State,
         [3]    which henceforth I wielded in ever-growing measure
            [4]    for five years and three months of world war,
                  at the end of which time,
         [5]    all our enemies having surrendered unconditionally
               or being about to do so,
[6]   I was immediately dismissed by the British electorate
               [7]    from all further conduct of their affairs. (*SWW,* I,
666)

While some find it pervaded by a sense of detachment and others by bitterness, everyone regards this a classic sentence.

Herbert Howarth shrewdly remarks of it that Churchill here is at once his father vindicated and his father dismissed, at once Caesar the victorious general and Caesar slain.[4]

That Churchill thought this an important sentence is indicated by his giving it a paragraph all to itself. (His paragraphs tend to be much longer.) Describing the climax of his life, the realization of his greatest dream and the occasion of one of his greatest disappointments, it moves with dignity and sweep. The lengthy relative clause ("[3] which ... I wielded ...") and the lengthy nominative absolute phrase ("[5] all our enemies ...") are framed by the two potent independent clauses ("[2] I acquired...," "[6] I was...") at either end of a sentence which describes what is for Churchill the main event at either end of the war. (The intervening years are, appropriately, disposed of by the middle of the sentence ["(4) for five years ... , at the end of which time"].) From the slow opening prepositional phrases ("[1] on the night ... , at the outset ..."), which are balanced by like phrases in the middle and at the end (4 and 7), the sentence gradually builds up in importance and thrust ("mighty," "chief power," "wielded," "ever-growing," "world war") until it reaches a dual climax ("enemies ... surrendered unconditionally," "dismissed ... electorate"), the latter part of which is really a terrible and ironic antithesis and anticlimax. "Immediately," contrasting with the five years discussed in five lines (and six volumes), is shocking; "dismissed" is a sorry coda to the series of words from "mighty" to "surrendered unconditionally." "Their affairs" adumbrates one of the last sentences of this vast work: "The verdict of the electors had been so overwhelmingly expressed that I did not wish to remain even for an hour responsible for their affairs" (*SWW*, VI, 675)—where "even for an hour" throws a heavy and bitter emphasis on "their" and where, in this indirect rebuke, Churchill says to the British as the banished, embittered Coriolanus had said to the Romans, "I banish you!"

The "tenth of May" sentence is not only charged with deeply personal feelings but also the climax of many of the major themes in Churchill's less personal writings. His readers are only too familiar with his ideas about elections, about the fickleness of the English populace, especially at war's end, about the surprising twists of life, especially political life, about the ordeals of great men, especially Churchills. They know that they are in the presence, in this most important of his prolepses, of a supreme example of these problems, that they confront what Churchill would take to be the final justification for his lifelong convictions. Thus this finely chiseled sentence presents, at once, the climactic phase in the career of the man of action, the classic instance of reversal recorded by the historian and ironist, and the consummate utterance of the artist-writer. He has scaled Mt. Olympus and on the heights forged a sentence which represents a great moment in the history of the West and of the sometimes curious democratic process and which contains, if words ever can, the quintessence of his labors and his writings.

The sentence, furthermore, has not one unnecessary word, not one false note (unless one wants to quibble over whether his power was indeed "ever-growing" during the war), not one imbalance. The narrator, speaking in the wake of a half-century of incredible political adventure, of numerous ups and downs, and of voluminous writing, tells of the supreme period of his life—and, by implication, of the glory and misery of mankind itself—with the calm finality and detachment (and perhaps the ghost of a sneer) of the Definitive Historian. Form and function are one; manner is wedded to matter. He has cast this most personal and painful of thoughts into an English sentence, which, he had once declared, is "a noble thing." Men have been great war leaders, and men have been turned out of office, but few have had the experiences out of which such thoughts might grow, fewer have survived to write about these experiences, and the fewest have had the verbal dexterity to conceive and order these brilliant words.

If in the realm of action, men will forgive Churchill much for the sake of 1940, so in the realm of composition the reader will overlook many flaws for the sake of that sentence and numerous others like it. In spite of considerable verbosity, self-glorification, and emotional self-indulgence pervading those eight million words and peeping forth even in some of the better passages quoted and praised in this study, Churchill will be called a stylist, a writer who has left his mark in the world of art.

CHAPTER 9

# "Whole Columns of Praise!": Reputation and Achievement

## I  Among British Historians

WHERE does Churchill stand in the line of British historians? With one of the earliest and greatest, Lord Clarendon, he shares the rare quality of being at once a man of action and writer, a mover first of men and then of words. Clarendon has a profounder mind, a more comprehensive vision, a greater sympathy, a more sinewy contemporary style, and a finer gallery of character portraits, but what Churchill may lack in quality vis-à-vis Clarendon, he compensates for with quantity, scope, narrative art, and occasional pithiness. He wrote a great deal more, on a larger range of topics and periods, with verve and with a larger number of memorable phrases and passages.

With many nineteenth-century historians, Churchill shares the Whig interpretation of history. This, as defined by Herbert Butterfield, involves siding with Protestants and Whigs, praising certain successful revolutions, emphasizing signs of progress in history, studying old events for the sake of the present, and seeing the past as ratifying the present. This approach imposes early nineteenth-century liberal values on the interpretation of history and regards the British monarchy as having been limited from time immemorial except for a brief period in the seventeenth-century (when Parliament, fortunately, brought back limited monarchy)—as against the Tory view (voiced most notably by David Hume) that the monarchy was absolute and that Parliament, not the Stuarts, broke the constitution and began the Civil War.

This Whig reading of events in part associates Churchill with one of the greatest nineteenth-century historians, Macaulay, who, like Clarendon and Churchill, had wide experience in parliamentary government and administration. He was the first English writer who made history universally interesting, more popular even than Scott's novels and poems, until Churchill came along. With Macaulay, Churchill shares a lush, oratorical style that sometimes becomes an end in itself, a preference for the portrayal of the dramatic events of history rather than the analysis of their origins, an inclination to portray individuals instead of currents and forces.

To both men, history is not just a collection of facts but requires the skills of the narrator and the painter. Both therefore tended to advocate rather than judge, to love exaggeration, caricature, and distortion, to misunderstand complex personalities, outsiders, mystics, and philosophers. Seeing life as a simple affair, cocksure in character and style, neither entertained the doubts of the speculative philosopher. Their theme is English superiority and English freedom, although Churchill was unable to share in the more blatant smugness that led Macaulay to pronounce his the most enlightened generation of the most enlightened of all peoples.

The adverse judgments now passed on Macaulay apply equally to Churchill: he is too sharp edged and lacking in subtle gradations; he is better at description than explanation; he is a humane and cultured philistine; blind to thought and emotion, he makes little effort to fathom the depths on which the pageantry of events floats like a foam; his wit and style come at the expense of the truth; his constant comparison of the past with the present is destructive of real historical knowledge; he is ignorant of countries and periods other than those he writes of; the bulk of his work is purely political history, mainly about Whig and Tory.

The charge that Macaulay and Churchill are disabled as historians by treating history as simply past politics is hardly peculiar to them. It has been leveled at the early nineteenth-century Catholic historian John Lingard and at S. R. Gardiner. And recently, the prominent historian Christopher Hill, in assigning G. R. Elton a secure place among the current leading English historians, complained of the absence in Elton's latest tome of exactly those things that scholars missed in Churchill's *History*—magic, medicine, literature, the arts, music, culture, social and economic forces, religion, and everyday life.

Another habit of Churchill's is traditional, that of relying heavily on documents that are meant to speak for themselves and to recapture the flavor of the times written about. Lingard, Gardiner, and C. H. Firth had a similar faith in the original sources, in letting the actors and witnesses set forth their opinions and arguments, and in making the reader live through the confusions and uncertainties of the changing course of events, rather than, as did Macaulay, giving a finished, seemingly definitive account.

These two approaches—the exclusively political and the documentary—come together in a work that may have influenced Churchill, John Morley's once highly acclaimed biography of Gladstone. Published in 1903, when Churchill was immersed in the biography of his own father, *Gladstone* is wholly limited to the subject's political career, with hardly a word about some of the subject's rather unusual personal interests (tree felling, attempting to reform prostitutes, studying classical literature). It is also rich in reproducing various documents, interlarded with explanations of the setting.

Like Carlyle, Churchill came dangerously close to hero worship, to seeing history altered by the thoughts and deeds of great men—albeit, unlike Carlyle, he characteristically limits himself to prominent military and political figures. He also seems, with Carlyle, at times to yoke together success and might, and to see in survival and triumph proof of moral worth.

Churchill resembled the American G. L. Beer in his vision of an English-speaking civilization, his pride in the spread of that civilization and in the development of the British Empire, his hope for a political reunion of America and Britain. Ignoring, like Beer, the contribution of non-British immigrants to America, Churchill said that Britons and Americans are essentially one and that there could be no hope for a world organization like the League unless like-minded people, such as the English-speaking one with their exemplary civilization, cooperated with each other and showed the way to mankind.

## II  *Reputation*

Churchill's reputation as a writer has not been independent of his reputation as a politician. In both fields, he has aroused strong and conflicting passions. His first books, like his first forays into the political forum, were greeted with acclaim as well as demurrals. *Malakand* and *River War* were very well received at the time of publication by literary and military critics as well as eminent Victorians; comparisons with Burke, Napier, and Disraeli were made. The books have since been, in the main, praised by historians as excellent examples of reportage, military-historical narrative, and, despite a certain lushness and literariness, amazingly mature style. But already annoyance was expressed over the author's "irrepressible egoism," "airs of infallibility," and his "cocksure criticism" of Kitchener. So also *Savrola*, his only novel, was seen as a literary sideshow or self-advertisement in the manner of Disraeli, and the Boer War books generated the observations that they force us to accept the fascinating, self-confident author at his own valuation, that they are romances with "the exposition of a remarkable personality" rather than scientific histories.[1]

Negative criticism was for once nearly swept aside by *Randolph Churchill*, which impressed contemporaries as a definitive, reverent, and perceptive literary and political masterpiece, a major biography written in a varied, poignant, calm prose. Although modern historians have pointed to suppressions of biographical data and insufficient comprehension of the larger historical currents and of the serious deficiencies of Randolph's character, the book has stood the test of time. Scholars and critics still praise it for its style, which is free of the Gibbon-Macaulay influence of the first books and the flamboyant rhetoric of the middle period works, for its masterly use of private papers, its grasp of the politics of the period, its maturity and judiciousness, its objectivity, its firm structure, its beautifully written drama—all noteworthy from so young an author.[2]

Between *Randolph Churchill* and Churchill's next major work, the *World Crisis*, lay two decades filled with numerous political and military disputes, not to speak of the egregious disaster of Gallipoli, so that anything Churchill would now write was certain to be controversial. Not surprisingly, therefore, *Blackwood's* anonymous reviewer of the first volume of the war memoirs turned the remarks on the Boer War books into severe censure. The new books was filled with "I, I, I," its author being the "most ferocious egoist of his time" who is at the center of every enterprise and who judges all men by whether they agree with him. Such a critique, or variations on it, were now often echoed. Other reviewers praised the work highly, and the response of more recent historians and critics has been ambivalent: much in it that is eloquent and valuable is confounded with bathos and claptrap.[3]

At this time Churchill's style underwent a change which critics complained of then and since. In the early decades he had been regarded as a literary craftsman among politicians, a professional writer of considerable stature, with a masculine sense of language and an unrivaled sense of form. While books or passages of his have been compared, for one reason or another, to the compositions of the biblical patriarchs and prophets, of Thycydides, Sallust, Cicero, Tacitus, Shakespeare, Clarendon, Addison, Swift, Dr. Johnson, Pitt, Scott, Thackeray, Carlyle, Trollope, Disraeli, Gladstone, Randolph Churchill, or Lytton Strachey, the greatest influence on him, at least in his early, formative period, has been acknowledged to be Gibbon and Macaulay. Churchill himself indicated in his autobiography that they were among the first writers he read when he undertook his self education and that they became models for him, Macaulay's style, with its "staccato antitheses," being crisp and forcible, Gibbon's, with its "rolling sentences and genetival endings" (*MEL*, 211), being stately and impressive.[4] That the first books, no less than the early speeches and interoffice memos, were influenced by the two was clear at once; reviewers complained of his exaggerated Gibbonian organ tone and Macaulayan false antitheses and forced emphases. Critics have differed as to whether one author or the other became the greater influence in the second book, the *River War*, but by the time of *Randolph Churchill*, he seems to have freed himself of most of the "Macaulay-Gibbon mummery."[5]

But now in the 1920s and 1930s Churchill was overtaken by what critics considered a baroque, flamboyant rhetoric. Many attributed it in part to the early influence of Gibbon and Macaulay, though not everyone thought that influence deleterious; some saw in the *World Crisis* Gibbonian "balance of thought" and Macaulayan "whirling passion." It seemed clear, moreover, as G. M. Trevelyan pointed out, that from Macaulay Churchill took, or with him he shared, a mystique of English history and the Whig interpretation of history; a public man's understanding of public events and an ability to narrate them clearly; a tendency to see things in black and white; an ebullience, self-centeredness, magnanimity, and a lack of psychology or subtlety.[6]

In the interwar period, furthermore, when his political career was erratic and his politics often Tory reactionary, the general attack upon an antebellum culture naturally injured someone writing in a style that, against the current of the age, actually grew in ornateness at this very time and that came to seem as archaic and petrified as his politics. If, therefore, Arthur Conan Doyle said of the *World Crisis* that it contained the "finest prose style of any contemporary" and some said that no English statesman was surer of a lasting place in literature—as the best of professional writers and as having a style shaped by the richest political vocabulary used with "instinctive felicity"—that indeed he was proficient mainly with words, not deeds, others dismissed him as a fossil. Herbert Read, in his influential *English Prose Style*, exhibited Churchill's lines on the Russian Revolution as a flagrant example of false eloquence, stale imagery, violent metaphors, childish dramatics, and bathos. (Even the "we shall fight" passage of 1940 struck him, in a postwar edition of his book, as inferior to Burke.) L. C. Knights, a prominent critic of English Renaissance literature, citing what he called a fraudulent passage in the *World Crisis* by a "modern journalist," dismissed the ghostly metaphors, glib phrases, empty verbiage, and diluted style as unacceptable anywhere except on the political platform and contrasted it with living and idiomatic Elizabethan prose.[7]

A notable exception to the style of the middle period is *A Roving Commission*, the short, personable autobiography written after the *World Crisis* and before *Marlborough*. Resembling, like Beethoven's Fourth Symphony, a slender Grecian maiden between two Norse giants, it took reviewers aback. Its informality, its cavalier tone, its retrospective, gay, gentle, wise humor—often directed at himself, or at least the younger self—seemed hardly to be from the same pen which wrote the sulfuric, defensive, dour, political, formal *World Crisis*. To many, this unlikely and brief effusion dashed off with the left hand has become, no doubt against the hopes and expectations of its author, more satisfying and durable than any of his numerous ambitious tomes.[8]

After the controversies surrounding the *World Crisis* (an entire book of hostile essays by military experts assailing its assumptions, statistics, and hypotheses was published in 1927), *Marlborough*, composed by a man "in the political wilderness" and in the apparent twilight of his career, received the sort of accolade which had been given *Randolph Churchill* three decades earlier. Yet there were animadversions against the book's obsession with wars, and historians have since noted the biographer's partiality for the hero and for Whig myths of history, his melodramatic, childish view of heroes and villains, his anachronistic reading of sociopolitical reality, his overripe style. But even with these faults, it remains to most critics a remarkable portrait of the age, written with balance, verve, intelligence, humor, mastery of language and structure.[9]

The *Second World War* received qualified praise. As in the case of its predecessor and sister work, the *World Crisis*, it struck critics as too deeply suffused with the author's self-importance. Clearly a selective account, defensive and self-serving, it yet has an unusual vantage point, a majesty and magnanimity, and its grand moments. Though it often contains more romance and oratory than historical exposition, though its awareness of the complexities of events is dim, it will long remain, with its rich documentation, a major work to be confronted by historians of the period. Its style, mingling gravity with humor, the lapidary with the informal, struck most critics as an improvement on that of the *World Crisis*. Notwithstanding its flaws, that a political leader could write so large and eloquent a work impelled reviewers into curious hyperbole. It was as if, according to the *Times Literary Supplement*, the *Iliad* had been written by Agamemnon or, according to the *American Historical Review*, Cromwell had written an epic in Milton's style or Frederick the Great in Goethe's. Although Lloyd George had made rather similar claims to uniqueness in his *War Memoirs*, Virginia Cowles is probably right in saying that no other great statesman or historian has had such a theme to match such a pen.[10]

While all of Churchill's books have sold well from the moment of publication, the *History*, like the *Second World War*, commanded an especially huge audience, because what the now legendary hero of 1940 had to say on any subject, let alone on the whole of Anglo-American history, was of great interest. Critical and scholarly response was more guarded. Historians found the work, notably its third volume, severely flawed by the author's narrow understanding of history as politics and war, his simplistic notions of good and evil, his Whig outlook, his patrician and English bias, his rhetoric of "liberty" and the British mission, his smug assumptions about a monolithic and superior English-speaking civilization, his antiquated scholarship, his primitive psychology and political science, his ignorance of sociology and philosophy, and his consequent obliviousness to historical forces. As always, the panoramic narrative of dramatic events (as against the analysis of long-range and less visible developments) is well handled, the character portraiture generous, the humor biting, the asides and aphorisms sage, the style glittering and, up to a point, persuasive. It will survive as a contribution to history by a successful man of action, politician, orator, journalist rather than a scholar.[11]

In the post-World War II period, the debate over Churchill's style has continued. Sympathetic and cogent defenses of it have been made by men of such stature as Isaiah Berlin, A. L. Rowse, H. S. Commager, and S. E. Morison. They do not regard its orotundity to be, as seemed in the interwar period, false, stale, self-aggrandizing, reactionary rhetoric, but expressive of Churchill's heroic, archaic, naive, but genuine vision. This vision, it had become evident, was precisely the element that had rallied his people in wartime adversity, and it imparted to his writings an excitement rare in professional historians. Others, however, persist in dismissing his writings as oral rhetoric rather than written literature. If the prominent historian H. S. Commager finds Churchill incapable of writing a dull paragraph, the authority on linguistics, Martin Joos, deprecates Churchill's "frozen style," which forces ideas on the reader and does not stimulate a rereading.[12]

One attempt to salvage something has been made by distinguishing an early period from the detours of the middle and from the somewhat chastened late period. This early style, as seen in his first speeches, no less than his first books, although influenced by the past, already shows the mature man's work, with its imagery, feeling, detail, majestic phrases, humor, and deliberate commonplace. Another approach would distinguish by genre rather than time, would separate the style of his memos, written in the heat of action, from the style of his books, written in periods of political inactivity, when the "artist" took over and indulged himself at leisure. He was so much the man of action rather than the writer that even the writing that is part of praxis is superior, or so goes the argument, to his pretentious literary-historical projects. Ronald Hyam speaks of the prose in Churchill's eloquent, cogent, precise early memos as containing some of his most forceful and trenchant writing and as expressing with "ruthless logic, foresight, polished phrases, arresting words" the thoughts of older colleagues better than they could themselves. So also Herbert Howarth finds the pungency, the "urgent imperious" English of the memos in the *Second World War* to be, especially when married to humor, above literature, while the bombast of the narrative style is beneath it.[13] To this genre criticism one might add the observation that the autobiographical journalism, like the *Roving Commission* which grew out of it, has a much more casual, humorous, humane tone than the solemn "official" works.

And if some emphasize his vast vocabulary and formal constructions as a major element of his great style, others, noting that such a style can go awry when applied to lesser matters (as in his travelogue, *My African Journey*), delight rather in the abrupt departures into the colloquial which characterize the journalistic pieces as well as the memos and certain speeches. They find unique in historical and political writing and oratory the judicious—and Shakespearean—mixture of the rhetorical and the cheeky, the ample and the brief, the dignified and the direct, the sonorous and the subdued, of Macaulay and slang, of Latin eloquence or *copia* and Anglo-Saxon pith or muscle; of a style, in short, in which someone writes from the political, social, and personal heights and yet makes personal contact with auditor and reader.[14]

The case against Churchill's style is often based on the assumption that ornateness is archaic in the twentieth century, but Louis Milic, citing the example of a Churchill or a Walter Lippmann, has plausibly argued that the ornate style is, like the plain, peculiar to no age and merely a rhetorical tendency present in all periods.[15] The matter can be clarified in another way. Francis Bacon distinguished between a "magistral" style—which is suasive and with which a knowing author imparts settled truths—and a "probative" or "initiative" style, in which an open-minded author, with no greater claim to the truth than his reader, explores and assays. The "magistral" style is characterized by symmetries and an authoritative tone, the "initiative" style by asymmetries, terseness, and, in reproducing the flow of thought in a mind sifting information and arriving at tentative hypotheses, loose connectives.

Written by someone imbued with a conservative sense of hierarchy, order, tradition, and Truth, as well as with an idiosyncratic, almost clinical, assurance of being personally right, Churchill's style is clearly "magistral," oratorical, didactic. "Far from echoing the rhythms of ordinary speech," says Walker Gibson, he "pontificates and chants in authoritarian rhythms" and "sounds like the wisdom of Moses," and some readers will argue that the "traditional manner lends sincerity and persuasiveness to the message."[16] In an age when oratory is suspect, however, and (in Yeats's words) "the best lack all conviction," the nervousness and tentativeness of the "probative" style seems to most readers closer to reality. Though this may be a judgment on us rather than on Churchill and though this may be merely a transitory phase, the fact remains that today's sensitive reader, raised on modern psychology, sociology, and philosophy, is simply not at ease with a style reflective of the credo which Churchill once explicitly stated and often implied: "At each stage the action which I took seemed right, natural, and even inevitable" (WC, I, 388).

## III  *Achievement*

Churchill's contribution as a writer is, therefore, bound to remain controversial. Despite much in them that seems faded now, his writings contain much else that is relevant and meaningful. Of such a nature are his emphases on sympathetic identification and on the importance of magnanimity; his healthy worship of political power in its democratic, beneficent form and his study of the different ways of using it in peace and especially war; his insider's view of the rise and fall of individual or party in a democracy, of the tragic and sordid as well as of the heroic and adventurous side of politics; his definitive articulation of the antipacifist, hawkish, Machiavellian approach to diplomacy. No less interesting are his commentaries on a series of major and minor wars, often based on firsthand observation; his study of the conditions and strategy of war and his understanding of the ever-increasing importance of technology in modern war; his healthy skepticism directed at the military bureaucracy and experts; his insistence on the importance of possessing a global vision and of being willing to take risks and losses, or at least of judging leniently those who do; his ability to separate the political scientist and military artist in Napoleon from the vain conqueror.

If he gives the classic, and to us lamentable, expression of the Victorian and early twentieth-century outlook on races and nations, with its sense of Western, white superiority, he yet offers an intelligent critique of the idea of progress, based on a sifting of the evidence. If he celebrates too much the virtues of patriotism, doing one's duty, indomitability, of fighting to the end for lost causes, he tells a gripping tale of the year, 1940, when such truisms became insights. If he is often complacent, vain, and blind in his judgments, he is equally, and inconsistently, aware of the ubiquity and mysteriousness of chance, the difficulties of pinpointing historical causation and fixing responsibility, indeed the superficiality of all historical judgments. However febrile or tendentious his writings are at times, Churchill will be read for his portrayal of some of the major figures and some of the dramatic scenes of history, many of which he knew at firsthand. Whatever the limitations of his style and technique or the deficiencies of his books, he has left on record a coherent view of early epochs of English history, a patrician picture of historical reality, a world view tenable with increasing difficulty—and rarely expressed with such eloquence since Burke—in a rapidly changing modern world.

The early books on the now insignificant frontier wars at the end of the last century, like, curiously, the unparalleled twelve large volumes of memoirs on the two cataclysmic world wars of our century, remain, if no longer definitive versions of the wars they describe, at least important primary works by a participant observer-journalist-chronicler. No historian of the wars they describe can afford to ignore them. Despite their flaws, the biographies of father and of ancestor come close to being definitive works and are likely to remain so for a long time, after necessary adjustments and qualifications have been made by later writers. The *History* was probably not intended to be anything but one amateur's and patriot's observations and essays on selected topics from English history. As such, far from being vulnerable to the tides of intellectual fashions, it is likely with the passage of time to take on greater interest and value—not, in other words, for the light it sheds on historical events but for the light these events, as interpreted by the author, shed on him. The shorter books and volumes of journalism—*A Roving Commission, Thoughts and Adventures, Great Contemporaries, Step by Step*—have never been denied style and literary quality as thorough, even if limited, studies in politics and character. Certain volumes of speeches—*Liberalism and the Social Problem, While England Slept, Blood, Sweat, and Tears*—remain powerful paeans to social reform, philippics against tyranny, and expressions of invincibility in the face of extreme adversity; they record Churchill's three great and entirely different heroic phases—as a Milton, a Demosthenes, and a Pitt.

Despite the unseemly self-dramatization, his story of one prominent man's role in many of the crises of the twentieth century, his fascinating if eccentric reading of the events of his epoch, has its literary as well as historical interests. The manner of the narrative is as compelling as the matter, thanks to his often poetic or novelistic imagery, his awareness of history, his agile use of the colloquial and the intimate no less than the literary and the Latinate vocabulary, of understatement, periphrasis, hyperbole, parallelism, antithesis, wordplay, zeugma, "as if" statements; his sustained and sparkling humor directed at idealism, religion, stupidity, at military and political men and mores, at self and, more frequently, political or national opponents; his ability with phrases, sentences, short passages; and his sustained effects, rhetorical or narrative.

Perhaps most important, the huge body of his writings is a tribute to the power of the written word and to the civilization in which a professional writer rather than a general became a leader and hero at a terrible juncture—and triumphed in good part by means of the word. It is also consoling evidence that, despite numerous depressing examples in our century, especially since Churchill's time, a politician may be literate, intelligent, articulate, individual, witty, charming; that, though rare in an age of speeches written by committees and memoirs by ghost writers, a blend of the political and literary crafts is perhaps still possible.

# Notes and References

## Chapter One

1. For a detailed study of his philosophy of composition, see my *Sword and Pen: A Survey of the Writings of Sir Winston Churchill* (Albuquerque, 1974), pp. 1-9, and my "Blood, Toil, Tears, and 8,000,000 Words: Churchill Writing," *Columbia Forum*, 4 (Spring, 1975), 19-23.

2. For one important aspect of his triumph in that year—his mastery of oratory and phrase making—see my "Churchill the Phrase Forger," *Quarterly Journal of Speech*, 68 (April, 1972), 161-74, and "Churchill as Orator: Wish and Fulfilment," *The Southern Speech Communication Journal*, 40 (Spring, 1975), 217-27.

## Chapter Two

1. Randolph Churchill, *Winston S. Churchill*, vol. 1 (Boston: Houghton Mifflin, 1967), pp. 343-44; *Companion Volume I* (Boston: Houghton Mifflin, 1968), Part 2, 804, 824, 864: *Companion Volume II*, Part 1, 454-60; Foreword, Cyril Clemens, *Mark Twain and David Eisenhower* (Webster Groves, Mo.: International Mark Twain Society, 1953). But he could not know of the volcanic late Twain, the writer of unpublished tracts attacking religion and patriotism in a mixture of Voltairean irony and Nietzschean wrath; he probably would have wondered what became of his hero had he encountered these works.

2. W. S. Blunt, *My Diaries*, 2 vols. (New York: Knopf, 1921), II, 298; Lord Moran, *Churchill* (Boston: Houghton Mifflin, 1966), pp. 439, 446, 457, 474, 517, 567, 581, 786, 789, 810, 813.

3. Randolph Churchill, I, 33; "Books in Your Life," *Coronet* 28 (May 1950), 64-65; Moran, pp. 281, 466.

4. Cf. GC, p. 135; Moran, p. 113.

5. *Companion Volume I*, Part 2, 858; *Strand*, May 1937, pp. 14ff.

6. PTO, 1 (June 16 and 23, 1906), pp. 25-27, 65-66; *Collier's*, August 22, 1936, pp. 22ff.; Moran, p. 158.

7. *News of the World*, January 8 to March 26, 1933, pp. 5-6.

8. He thought (in 1912) the *Oedipus the King* a fine play but

would not rush to see it again (see *Companion Volume II*, Part 3, 1499).

9. It was poetic justice therefore that in H. G. Wells's attack on Churchill, the novel *Men Like Gods*, the same scene in *Paradise Lost* is alluded to, with Churchill himself as Satan plotting hellish attack against the gentle Utopians. Since *Men Like Gods* antedates this volume of the *World Crisis*, one wonders whether Churchill is consciously retaliating.

### Chapter Three

1. *Collier's*, May 4, 1935, pp. 22ff.
2. *Strand Magazine*, January, 1936, pp. 276-86.
3. For a full discussion of the complex question of Churchill's politics, see my "Churchill and Conservatism," *Southern Humanities Review*, 10 (Winter, 1976), 43-54.
4. *Strand Magazine*, March, 1933, pp. 246-55.
5. This problem is discussed at length in my "Churchill and the 'Great Man' Theory of History," *Connecticut Review*, 8 (October, 1974), 20-35.

### Chapter Four

1. *London Magazine*, October, 1916, p. 120; December, 1916, pp. 395ff. Cf. also the later Churchill's skeptical remark on medical experts: "the fashionable fallacies of the Royal physicians" (in *Collier's*, May 15, 1937, p. 12).
2. *News of the World*, March 10, 1935, p. 5.
3. Introduction, Richard Bermann, *The Mahdi of Allah* (London, 1931), pp. xi-xiv; *Sunday Pictorial*, April 8, 1917, p. 5.
4. *London Magazine*, November, 1916, pp. 235ff; *Collier's*, October 7, 1939, pp. 12ff.
5. For a detailed analysis of the portrayal of Marlborough and the implicit self-portrayal, see my forthcoming "Churchill and Marlborough."
6. *Collier's*, October 7, 1939, pp. 62-3; ATS, p. 157.
7. *Illustrated Sunday Herald*, May 30, 1920, p. 5.
8. Foreword, *War Speeches of William Pitt*, sel. R. Couland (Oxford, 1940).

### Chapter Five

1. Martin Gilbert, *Winston S. Churchill*, vol. 5 (Boston, 1977), pp. 287, 436; Harold Nicolson, *Diaries and Letters*, ed. N. Nicolson, 3 vols. (London, 1966-1968), II, 279.
2. *Collier's*, July 11, 1936, pp. 21ff; August 13, 1932, pp. 20ff;

*Daily Telegraph*, December 2, 1929, p. 10; *News of the World*, September 4, 1938, p. 12.

3. *Evening Standard*, May 6, 1935, p. 12.

4. Gilbert, V, 278, 972.

5. The relevant passages in Machiavelli are: *The Prince*, chaps. 3, 8, 12, 17, 19, 21; *The Discourses*, Bk I, chaps. 6, 16, 22, 26-27, 30, 34, 38, 51; Bk II, chaps. 14-15, 18, 23, 30; Bk. III, chaps. 2, 37, 40 (in Max Lerner's 1940 Modern Library edition, pp. 9, 11, 14, 35, 44, 60, 63, 83-85, 129, 163, 173, 177, 184-86, 193, 203, 214, 243, 321, 323, 343, 358, 387, 404, 521, 527). Cf. also John Adams: "In politics, the middle way is none at all."

## Chapter Six

1. For a detailed analysis of the major theme peculiar to each of Churchill's four major works, as well as of their interrelationships, see *Sword and Pen*, pp. 78-88, 120-25, 158-68, 189-99, 221-27.

2. *Scribner's Magazine*, December, 1930, pp. 587-97; *Saturday Review* (London), February 15, 1896, p. 165, and March 7, 1896, p. 22.

3. Speeches of February 8 and March 18, 1912.

4. *Collier's*, May 4, 1935, pp. 22, 30.

5. *Sunday Pictorial*, January 12, 1919, p. 5.

6. For a detailed study of Churchill's not always unqualified worship of the United States and his—actually antiquated—dream of an English-speaking association, see my "America Through Churchill's Eyes," *Thought*, 50 (March, 1975), 5-34.

## Chapter Seven

1. Introduction to Bermann, *The Mahdi of Allah*, pp. xi-xiv.

2. *Collier's*, January 4, 1947, pp. 11ff.

3. *Scribner's Magazine*, December, 1930, pp. 587-97. Cf. such journalistic exercises as "If We Could Look Into the Future!" and "If I Were An American."

4. For praise and criticism by professional philosophers of Churchill's ventures into hypothetical speculation, See C. E. M. Joad, in Eade, pp. 475-89, and Sidney Hook, *The Hero in History* (1943; rpt. Boston, 1967), pp. 117, 128-35.

5. Weekly Dispatch, October 5, 1924, p. 8.

## Chapter Eight

1. *Saturday Evening Post*, February 15, 1930, p. 25.

2. *Life*, April 14, 1947, p. 12.

3. Winston Weathers, in *Contemporary Essays on Style*, ed. Glen Love and Michael Payne (Glenview, Ill., 1969), p. 24.

4. Herbert Howarth, "Behind Churchill's Grand Style," *Commentary*, 11 (1951), 554. See also Virginia Cowles, *Churchill* (New York, 1953), p. 355, and Harold Nicolson, *Diaries and Letters*, ed. Nigel Nicolson, 3 vols. (New York, 1966-1968), III, 33.

## Chapter Nine

1. Randolph Churchill, *Winston S. Churchill*, vol. 1 (Boston, 1966), pp. 367, 442-43, 499; Compton Mackenzie, G. W. Price, and Colin Coote, in Eade, pp. 50, 80, 178-82; H. S. Commager, "Preface," in Winston Churchill, *Marlborough* (New York, 1968), pp. xxiii-xxiv; J. H. Plumb, "The Historian," in *Churchill Revised* (New York, 1969), pp. 156-59; D. C. Somervell, "Sir Winston Churchill," in *Nobel Prize Winners*, ed. E. J. Ludovici (London, 1956), pp. 7-8; R. R. James, *Churchill* (London, 1970), pp. 6, 27; Maurice Ashley, *Churchill As Historian* (New York, 1968), pp. 39, 51; Peter de Mendelssohn, *The Age of Churchill* (New York, 1961), pp. 109, 141-47, 192; Philip Guedella, *Mr. Churchill* (New York, 1942), pp. 69, 109; A. L. Rowse, "Sir Winston Churchill As An Historian," in *The English Spirit*, rev. ed. (New York, 1966), p. 80; L. G. Brock, in *The Bookman* (December, 1900), p. 87; Anon., in *American Historical Review*, 12 (1906), 303.

2. Anon., *Edinburgh Review*, 204 (July, 1906), 1-34; Anon., *The Bookman* (July, 1908), p. 137; R. R. James, *Lord Randolph Churchill* (New York, 1960), pp. 11, 13, 371; Plumb, pp. 145-48; de Mendelssohn, p. 301; Ashley, pp. 55-56, 68; Cowles, p. 110; Rowse, pp. 79-80; Commager, pp. xx, xxii; Guedella, pp. 107, 109; Malcolm Muggeridge, "Churchill the Biographer and Historian," in Eade, pp. 346-47.

3. Anon., *Blackwood's Magazine*, 214 (December, 1923), 868-73; Ashley, pp. 69, 73, 102-4; James, *Churchill*, pp. 31, 351; Plumb, p. 163; Moran, p. 348; Muggeridge, p. 349; Rowse, p. 79; Samuel J. Hurwitz, "Winston S. Churchill," in *Some Modern Historians of Britain*, ed. H. Ausubel et al. (New York, 1951), p. 314.

4. What exactly he borrowed and how successfully is a matter of debate. While he clearly learned formality, balance, and judicious choice of words from them, some critics believe that he actually imitated neither but forged his own style, and others found that his style is cluttered with superlatives and adjectives which the masters would have eschewed; borrowing from them only the surface, he preferred ostentation, indiscrimination, and vague magnificence in place of their exactitude. See, e.g., Plumb, p. 144; Howarth, p. 550; Coote, in Eade, p. 80. But one might remember the "startled gods" sentence in

the *River War*, which showed that, if the Gibbon-Macaulay style sometimes served Churchill as a substitute for thinking, it at other times sharpened his perception.

5. Randolph Churchill, I, 443, 499; Ronald Hyam, *Elgin and Churchill at the Colonial Office 1905-08* (London, 1968), pp. 493, 501-3; H. L. Stewart, *Sir Winston Churchill As Writer and Speaker* (London, 1954), p. 40; Somervell, p. 7; Guedella, p. 69; de Mendelssohn, p. 301; Anon., in *Times Literary Supplement*, January 28, 1965, p. 67. The phrase is de Mendelssohn's.

6. Plumb, pp. 141, 163: John Connell, *Winston Churchill*, Writers and Their Work, no. 80 (London, 1956), pp. 22-23; Somervell, p. 17; G. M. Trevelyan, *England Under Queen Anne*, 3 vols. (London, 1931-1934), I, 178; III, xiii.

7. James, *Churchill*, p. 185; Herbert Read, *English Prose Style* (1928; rpt. Boston, 1952), pp. 171-72; L. C. Knights, in *Perspectives on Style*, ed. F. Candelaria (Boston, 1968), pp. 197-99, 207. Churchill was not alone; Bonamy Dobree (in *Modern Essays on Writing and Style*, ed. Paul Wermuth [New York, 1964], p. 143) in 1934 took G. M. Trevelyan to task for using archaic devices in his narrative on Marlborough, the very devices which Churchill was still using a few years later in *his* book on Marlborough.

8. Anon. in *Times Literary Supplement*, October, 23, 1930, p. 851; T. H. Thomas in *Journal of Modern History* (1931), p. 512; Cowles, p. 278; Plumb, p. 159; Guedella, p. 247; James, *Churchill*, pp. 313-14.

9. Plumb, pp. 149-54; James, *Churchill*, pp. 312-13; Stewart, pp. 64, 66-74; Cowles, p. 290; Rowse, pp. 79, 82-83; Guedella, p. 250; Ashley, pp. 156-57; Commager, pp. xx, xxix-xxxi.

10. Plumb, p. 166; Reed Whittemore, in *Language and Politics*, ed. T. P. Brockway (Boston, 1965), pp. 63-67; Isaiah Berlin, *Mr. Churchill in 1940* (London, 1949), pp. 14-15, 39; Ashley, pp. 160, 192-93, 207-9; Muggeridge, pp. 348-51; Stewart, p. 138; Connell, pp. 31, 35-37; James, *Churchill*, pp. 221-22, 278; Commager, pp. xx, xxiv; *TLS*, April 30, 1954, p. 273; *AHR*, 54 (1949), p. 858; Cowles, p. 362.

11. Plumb, pp. 152-53; Rowse, pp. 79, 85-91; Gordon K. Lewis, "Mr. Churchill As Historian," *The Historian*, 20 (August, 1958), pp. 390-413; Ashley, pp. 210-11, 215-23; James, *Churchill*, pp. 310-12.

12. Berlin, p. 8; James, *Churchill*, pp. 310, 316; Howarth, pp. 549-50; Connell, p. 10; Guedella, pp. 223, 250; H. S. Commager, Preface to Winston Churchill, *A History of the English-Speaking Peoples* (New York, 1965), p. vi; Martin Joos, *The Five Clocks* (New York, 1961), p. 49. For a psychological explanation (insecurity) see Anthony Storr, "The Man," in *Churchill Revised*, p. 268, and for a practical explanation (dictation), see Plumb, pp. 144, 163.

13. Hyam, pp. 115-17, 493, 501-3; de Mendelssohn, pp. 218, 301,

342; Cowles, p. 85; James, *Churchill*, pp. 28, 310; Guedella, p. 69; Howarth, p. 556.

14. See, e.g., Berlin, p. 13; Guedella, pp. 116-17; Ivor Brown, in Eade, pp. 453-58; Anon., *Times Literary Supplement*, July 1, 1949, p. 422.

15. Louis Milic, in S. Chatman and S. R. Levin, *Essays in the Language of Literature* (Boston, 1967), pp. 448-49.

16. Walker Gibson, in Wermuth, p. 254; on Bacon's distinction see S. Fish and E. I. Berry, in *Seventeenth-Century Prose*, ed. Stanley Fish (New York, 1971), pp. 259, 299-300.

# Selected Bibliography

## PRIMARY SOURCES

*The Story of the Malakand Field Force.* London: Longmans, Green, 1898 *(MFF)*.

*The River War.* 2 vols. London: Longmans, Green, 1899 *(RW)*.

*London to Ladysmith via Pretoria.* London: Longmans, Green, 1900 *(L)*.

*Ian Hamilton's March.* London: Longmans, Green, 1900 *(IH)*.

*Savrola.* 1900; rpt. New York: Random House, 1956 *(S)*.

*Lord Randolph Churchill.* 2 vols. New York: Macmillan, 1906 *(RC)*.

*For Free Trade.* London: Humphreys, 1906 *(FFT)*.

*My African Journey.* London: Hodder and Stoughton, 1908 *(AJ)*.

*Liberalism and the Social Problem.* 2d ed. London: Hodder and Stoughton, 1909 *(LSP)*.

*The People's Rights.* London: Hodder and Stoughton, 1910 *(PR)*.

*The World Crisis.* 6 vols. New York: Scribner's, 1923-1931 *(WC)*.

*A Roving Commission: My Early Life.* New York: Scribner's, 1930 *(MEL)*.

*India.* London: Thornton Butterworth, 1931 *(Ind)*.

*Amid These Storms (Thoughts and Adventures).* New York: Scribner's, 1932 *(ATS)*.

*Great Contemporaries.* New York: Putnam's, 1937 *(GC)*.

*Marlborough, His Life and Times.* 4 vols. 1933-1938; rpt. 2 vols. London: Harrap, 1947 *(M)*.

*While England Slept (Arms and the Covenant).* New York: Putnam's, 1938 *(WES)*.

*Step by Step: 1936-1939.* New York: Putnam's, 1939 *(SbS)*.

*Blood, Sweat, and Tears (Into Battle).* New York: Putnam's, 1941 *(BST)*.

*The Unrelenting Struggle.* London: Cassell, 1942 *(US)*.

*The End of the Beginning.* Boston: Little, Brown, 1943 *(EoB)*.

*Onwards to Victory.* Boston: Little, Brown, 1944 *(OtV)*.

*The Dawn of Liberation.* London: Cassell, 1945 *(DoL)*.

*Victory.* Boston: Little, Brown, 1946 *(Vi)*.

*Secret Session Speeches.* London: Cassell, 1946 *(SSS)*.

*The Second World War.* 6 vols. Boston: Houghton Mifflin, 1948-1953 *(SWW)*.

*The Sinews of Peace.* Boston: Houghton Mifflin, 1949 *(SoP)*.

*Europe Unite.* Boston: Houghton Mifflin, 1950 *(EU)*.

*In the Balance*. Boston: Houghton Mifflin, 1952 (*ItB*).
*Stemming the Tide*. Boston: Houghton Mifflin, 1954 (*StT*).
*A History of the English-Speaking Peoples*. 4 vols. 1956-1958; rpt.
   New York: Bantam, 1963 (*HESP*).
*The Unwritten Alliance*. London: Cassell, 1961 (*UA*).

### SECONDARY SOURCES

ASHLEY, MAURICE. *Churchill As Historian*. New York: Scribner's,
   1968. Useful on the question of Churchill's accuracy.
BERLIN, ISAIAH. *Mr. Churchill in 1940*. London: John Murray, 1949.
   Sympathetic interpretation of style and sensibility.
COMMAGER, HENRY STEELE, ed. *Marlborough*. New York: Scribner's,
   1968. Pp. xix-xxxiii. An eminent historian's eloquent tribute to
   Churchill's strengths as a writer.
CONNELL, JOHN. *Winston Churchill*. Writers and Their Work, no. 80.
   London: Longmans, Green, 1956. A good survey.
DEAKIN, F. W. "Churchill the Historian." *Schweitzer Monatshefte*,
   49 (1969-1970). Some helpful observations by a former re-
   searcher.
HOWARTH, HERBERT. "Behind Churchill's Grand Style." *Commen-
   tary*, 11 (1951), 549-57. Best expression of the viewpoint that
   Churchill was less historian or stylist than windbag.
HURWITZ, SAMUEL J. "Winston S. Churchill." In *Some Modern Histo-
   rians of Britain*, edited by H. Ausubel et al. New York: Dryden,
   1951. Pp. 306-24. Good critical survey, with negative conclu-
   sions.
LEWIS, GORDON K. "Mr. Churchill As Historian." *The Historian*, 20
   (August, 1958), 387-414. The most searching and acute analysis
   of Churchill's limitations.
MAGEE, BRYAN. "Churchill's Novel" *Encounter*, 25 (October, 1965),
   45-51. Excellent analysis of *Savrola*.
MUGGERIDGE, MALCOLM. "Churchill the Biographer and Historian."
   In *Churchill By His Contemporaries*, edited by Charles Eade.
   London: Hutchinson, 1953. Pp. 343-53. Good discussion of
   Churchill's failings as a writer.
PLUMB, J. H. "The Historian" In *Churchill Revised*. New York: Dial,
   1969. Pp. 131-69. One of the best essays; excellent on Churchill's
   blinkers.
ROWSE, A. L. "Sir Winston Churchill As An Historian" In *The En-
   glish Spirit*. Rev. ed. New York: Funk and Wagnall's, 1966. Pp.
   78-92. Somewhat reverent and chatty praise of the *Marlborough*
   and the *History*.
WEIDHORN, MANFRED. *Sword and Pen: A Survey of the Writings of
   Sir Winston Churchill*. Albuquerque: University of New Mexico

Press, 1974. The first full-length study of the evolution of Churchill's thinking, of his state of mind in each of six phases; concentrates on his five major works.

WHITTEMORE, REED. "Churchill and the Limitations of Myth." In *Language and Politics*, edited by T. P. Brockway. Boston: D. C. Heath, 1965. Pp. 56-68. Excellent detailed analysis of Churchill's solipsism in the *Second World War*.

# Index